SECOND
STORY
Press

820
.809
287
Eye

7355

Eye to eye : women : their words and worlds. Life in
Africa, Asia, Latin America and the Caribbean as seen
in photographs and in fiction by the region's top
women writers / [edited by Vanessa Baird]. --
Canadian ed. --Toronto : Second Story Press,
1997, c1996.
127 p. : ill. (chiefly col.)

856901   ISBN:1896764002 (pbk.)

(SEE NEXT CARD)
94   97DEC18   3559/he   1-490752

– for my mother –

eye to eye

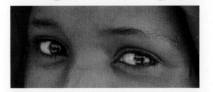

women

eye to eye
women

*Their words and worlds.
Life in Africa, Asia, Latin America and the
Caribbean as seen in photographs and in
fiction by the region's top women writers.*

CANADIAN CATALOGUING IN PUBLICATION DATA

Main entry under title:

Eye to eye: women

ISBN 1-896764-00-2

1. African literature (English) – Women authors. 2. African literature (English).
3. Caribbean literature (English) – Women authors. 4. Caribbean literature
(English). 5. Latin American literature (English) – Women authors.
6. Latin American literature (English). 7. Oriental literature (English) –
Women authors. 8. Oriental literature (English). 9. Women – Literary
collections. I. Baird, Vanessa.

PN6069.W65E93 1997   820.8'09287   C96-932606-8

First published in Great Britain by
New Internationalist Publications Ltd,
55 Rectory Road, Oxford OX4 1BW

Designed by Barbara Willi-Halter for New Internationalist Publications

Printed by C&C Offset Printing Co. Ltd., Hong Kong.

Canadian edition 1997
SECOND STORY PRESS
720 Bathurst Street Suite 301
Toronto, Canada
M5S 2R4

– contents –

love and life

work and play

culture and creativity

environment

politics and society

endpiece

IT WAS PURE *pleasure – reading through some of the most vibrant writing by women from Africa, Asia, Latin America and the Caribbean and matching it with some of the most stunning images from the* NEW INTERNATIONALIST *stock of photographs.*

It was tricky though. The basic considerations were simple enough: first and foremost, the writing and the images had to be of high quality. Then the subject matter and the geographic region had to match. But having got that far, if you then found that the mood and atmosphere of the text jarred with that of the picture, well, then the match simply didn't work. The perfect moment was when the words and the image worked together in an expressive duet of both literary and visual power.

We – designer Barbara Willi-Halter and I – started with literally hundreds of pictures and texts, from a wide range of writers and photographers. Some of the writers were well known – others less so. Some of the photographs may also be known to you – classics from the World Calendars and Almanacs produced by NEW INTERNATIONALIST *Publications in the UK, in conjunction with Barbara Willi-Halter and Helvetas in Switzerland, and other European partners. My colleague Dinyar Godrej provided an invaluable second opinion.*

The idea behind this collection is to bring to a wider audience some of the most vivid contemporary writing from women in Africa, Asia, Latin America and the Caribbean – the so-called Majority World. It is difficult enough for writers from these regions to get their work published and disseminated in a world dominated by the wealth and values of Western industrialized nations. For women writers from the Majority World it has been doubly hard.

In Latin America, says best-selling Chilean novelist Isabel Allende, writing was 'a man's game' until only very recently. 'The world was run by men and written about by men who, consequently, wrote us, our role and our place in their world.'

But now, according to Allende, women have 'stormed the literary bastions en masse and seized the right to write themselves, define themselves'. As a result characterizations of women have become more varied: 'We have broken out of the stereotypical scheme of madonnas, child-women and whores to portray real human beings, rebellious, anxious, concerned, advancing together – women that love, fear, and hate,' says Allende.

The same could be said of women writing today in Africa, Asia and the Caribbean – although the degree to which women have managed to 'storm the literary bastions en masse' in all these regions is open to question. African women writers have found it particularly difficult to break onto the literary scene.

While feminist publishing houses in Europe or North America have provided outlets for many new Western women writers, such publishing ventures are still a rare phenomenon in the Southern hemisphere. Exceptions do exist though – such as India's remarkable Kali for Women, set up in New Delhi in 1984 and still going strong. The efforts of publishers like these and their more outward-looking co-publishing partners in the North have done much to bring Southern women's writing to an appreciative international audience.

Things are changing, as this selection shows. Some of the authors included are already internationally renowned – and the extracts here may serve to remind you what interesting writers they are. Others you may never have heard of – and I hope you enjoy the thrill of discovering their work as much as I did.

To the more literary-minded, the logic of including photographs in a collection of prose and poetry may be puzzling. But, apart from looking good, the pictures have something of a cultural translation function in providing an immediate visual context. For example, an African author writing for an African readership may not consider it necessary to describe the kind of clothes her characters wear or the kind of houses they live in. But for the reader sitting in Arkansas or Amsterdam or Adelaide it might actually increase their enjoyment of the piece if they can visualize such details. The all-inclusive eye of the camera lens does the trick.

This book could serve to introduce you to people and experiences neglected by dint of geography and gender. But above all it's for you to enjoy – enjoy the energy, variety, eloquence and sheer imaginative power of the women who have contributed to it.

The journey begins with an introduction from award-winning Indian novelist Anita Desai – a thoughtful guide if ever there was one – who lights the way with her gentle and illuminating insights.

Vanessa Baird

Vanessa Baird, Oxford, 1996

I WENT TO Queen Mary's School for Girls in the sleepy neighbourhood of Old Delhi where I grew up, and was taught all subjects, including mathematics and what we called 'PT' by women. The only men on the premises were a mild-mannered turbaned Sikh who sold us stationery and textbooks and, for some reason, our Hindi teacher, a shy, awkward, bespectacled man whose courage in stepping into this feminine enclave awed me even at the time. When I went on to a women's college at the University of Delhi I was taught by another battery of women teachers, splendid and memorable creatures all, who suffered with a saintly tolerance and good humour the rebellious phases of their students and wards. A year after I graduated I married and for the first time entered a world run and controlled by men. It was a great shock.

Not an uncommon experience for women of my generation, and my contemporaries dealt with it in different ways: some became teachers of the same mould as those who had taught them; others took to social service and organizational work with a zeal I could never attempt to emulate; others married and raised children, as I did; each making their own adjustments, compromises, engagements and advances – as best they could.

My way had been writing ever since I mastered the alphabet: seeing how letters and words ordered themselves on a page, created patterns and had reason and logic and craft, yet left spaces for the imagination to fill. I saw how the chaos of life, too, could be placed on paper so that it yielded sense and meaning. I am not prepared to go further than this in the analysis of the creative impulse but will not be surprised if others see in it the desire to take control of one's world, a desire that is matched with the urge to tell the truth, tell it as one sees and experiences it.

These desires cannot so easily be equated with the creative aspects of nature although the affinity of women with nature (and peace, and the body, and the unconscious) has been evoked so often as to become a cliché. To read this collection of writing by women in the non-Western world does, to some extent, reiterate the ancient beliefs in female power, in the nature of a woman's love and a mother's role.

The section *Life and Love*, for instance, will prove that if love described by a male writer has been commonly sexual love between the sexes, then the love described by women writers – such as Mariama Bâ, Alifa Rifaat and Shashi Deshpande – is as often love between mother and daughter, grandmother and grandchild, or childhood friends. The force of physical love is present here too – in Omega Agüero's prose and Fahmida Riaz's poetry – but there is a greater inclusiveness. The world described here is wider, not narrower. And there is an added dimension, one that can only be called 'political', because once love is submitted to social form – marriage, for example – then everything is subtly altered and the differences are most striking. Nawal El Saadawi highlights this difference in a witty piece in →

which both man and woman make passionate protestations of love but, depending on which sex is making them, their protestations yield very different meanings. So, yes, one will find here that traditional, ancient and accepted link between female power and creativity – 'the eternal feminine' – and the equation between feminine nature and the environment. Aman celebrates the birth of a child in the desert, linking it – both literally and metaphorically – with rainfall that makes the desert flower: 'A lot of different flowers were there, flowers that nobody planted – Allah planted – white ones, red ones, purple ones – wild flowers all around them. Everything turned green and life was back to normal.' Anees Jung writes of the centrality of the ancestral village and lands even in the lives of urbanized Indians making a living in the metropolises; and Luisa Valenzuela describes the communication in a small village high up in the Andes, so subtle that it is a matter of silences rather than speech, and an attitude to time exemplified by an absence of conjugations, there being no notion of time past or future, only of time now and always. There is a sense of peace and harmony and continuity about these ideas that is pleasing and reassuring – although the rhythms of Assumpta Acam-Oturu's poem *Arise to the Day's Toil* are likely to drum a different message into ones ears if one listens.

Certainly less peaceful and harmonious is the relationship of the female sex with authority and its ordained structures – altogether a more fraught and problematic matter. In the section on *Politics and Society* we find women scrutinizing their traditional place in society and finding it considerably less than satisfying or fair: the girl children in Mrinal Pande's story learn young that they hold a position inferior to the sons of the family; the seven-year-old girl Kebbedesh discovers that when she runs away after being raped by her elderly husband she is no longer wanted by her family and that the only means of survival she has is prostitution. Society is depicted everywhere as rigid, adamantine in its structure, so that no-one, no matter how impassioned, logical or clear-thinking, can dislodge its conventions. The roles of the sexes appear to be written in stone, so that even if a girl is beautiful, gifted and blameless, Suniti Namjoshi tells us: 'Everyone in the village was critical of her. "To be so damned good," they said, "is not womanly".'

To become aware is to resist, and there is no dumb acceptance to be found here. Instead we see an eagerness to contest the state, the situation, a willingness to engage with it, however bruising and battering such an encounter might be. The perpetually pregnant heroine of Andrée Chedid's story begs the holy man to remove his 'benediction' and put a stop to the flood of children she is 'blessed' with, but meets with his contempt and abuse. This is only realistic, and the neo-realism of much fiction written by women has played an important role in 'consciousness raising' across the world, from the United States to China. Lacking support from other quarters women have proved capable of helping themselves, sometimes through private →

and even secret subterfuges and subversions as the mother does in Alifa Rifaat's *An Incident in the Ghobashi Household* to protect her unmarried, pregnant daughter, or by joining together to oppose the state and its tyrannies as Ester does in the search she organizes for the missing children of Guatemala, or of helping each other like the women who come to the aid of Kebbedesh and provide her with a sewing machine so that she can become, finally, self-sufficient.

Ignorance
Shattered us into fragments
we had to unearth ourselves piece by piece
to recover with our own hands such
unexpected relics

Abena Busia writes in her poem *Liberation*. Ignorance and isolation are acknowledged as the weakening factors and there is a passionate belief in learning, in the power of education, that one might expect in those who have been traditionally deprived of it; but the belief in its power is not naive, not simplistic. Domitila Barrios de Chungara in *Let Me Speak* expresses this ambivalence: she speaks with pride of her father who insisted on raising his daughters as he would have his sons, and of a schoolteacher who helped her along, but adds:
'I can't say that school really helped me to understand life. I think that education... is still a part of the capitalist system we live in... In school they teach us to sing the national anthem, to parade... they never explain our poverty, our misery, our parents' situation, their great sacrifice and low wages, why a few children have everything and many others have nothing. They never explained that in school...'
And from the emphasis given, it is clear that is what she wants to learn. Nor did Jung Chang in *Wild Swans* find that to be given a place in a man's world made her a man. A new life with *The Electrician's Manual* simply gave her a great many jolts – electric ones – but left her essentially as she was since she was allowed little choice. Choices had been made for her, and all that was left for her to do was fit into the new society created by the Cultural Revolution in China.

The same wisely wary attitude towards established institutions is revealed with regard to what is generally taken to be a woman's natural domain: religion. The women we meet in this collection seem quite aware of, and suspicious of, its patriarchal cast, as the desperate woman in Andrée Chedid's story is when she rails against the holy man. They deal with it by giving it a twist or a turn, manipulating it or recasting it to fit their needs, as voodoo appears to do in Clarice Lispector's *The Hour of the Star*.

What is apparent in any such engagement is that women are nowhere passive, helpless, despairing beings crushed by patriarchy. They are sometimes accomplices; at other times manipulators; what they seem to intuit early and everywhere is that the system must be subverted if one is not to bruise oneself by beating →

one's head against its stone walls. Therefore, even in the most consciously 'literary' pieces of prose and poetry here, there is a refusal to conform, a refusal to accept or imitate. Instead, a buzzing, seething, heaving, stirring sense of restless questioning, of unsatisfied and urgent desires and controlled energy gives us a rapidly moving picture instead of a static and timeless scene. Goddesses and sorceresses are known, after all, to be capable of myriad transformations and transmutations, surviving by disappearing and by unexpectedly reappearing. So the collection has about it an air of bustle, of being up and on the move which anyone who has ever been present when a house is being turned upside down and cleaned, or in a kitchen when a meal is being whipped up, or in a roomful of babies all needing to be nursed, fed, bathed, dressed, taught and instructed, will instantly recognize.

Writing too is women's work, after all...

Anita Desai, Massachusetts, 1996

PASSIONS TENDER, PASSIONS TURBULENT. Love arouses a myriad of emotions. From Pakistani poet Fahmida Riaz's warm glow of total fulfilment to Cuban story-teller Omega Agüero's ardent fury of frustration. From the slow, deep, lasting love of a close friendship between two women, friends since childhood, to the sudden, *love and life* dizzying madness that's sexual enchantment. From the complicity of love and loyalty between mother and daughter — to the realization that some expectations will never be met. Then, of course, there are the lying charades demanded by convention, from a very tongue-in-cheek Nawal El Saadawi.

– an intimate
friendship recalled
by Mariama Bâ –

dEAR AISSATOU,
I have received your letter. By way of reply, I am beginning this diary, my prop in my distress. Our long association has taught me that confiding in others allays pain.

Your presence in my life is by no means fortuitous. Our grandmothers in their compounds were separated by a fence and would exchange messages daily. Our mothers used to argue over who would look after our uncles and aunts. As for us, we wore out wrappers and sandals on the same stony road to the koranic school; we buried our milk teeth in the same holes and begged our fairy godmothers to restore them to us, more splendid than before. If over the years, and passing through the realities of life, dreams die, I still keep intact my memories, the salt of remembrance.

I conjure you up. The past is reborn, along with its procession of emotions. I close my eyes. Ebb and tide of feeling: heat and dazzlement, the woodfires, the sharp green mango, bitten into in turns, a delicacy in our greedy mouths. I close my eyes. Ebb and tide of images: drops of sweat beading your mother's ochre-coloured face as she emerges from the kitchen; the procession of young wet girls chattering on their way back from the springs.

We walked the same paths from adolescence to maturity, where the past begets the present. ◆

from **SO LONG A LETTER**
by Mariama Bâ, Senegal

Friends share a rare treat of ice cream – and less tangible pleasures – in Southern Algeria.

Photo: C. Eykeman

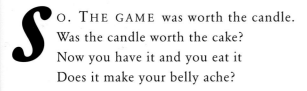

*– Jane King's ditty
on infidelity –*

SO. THE GAME was worth the candle.
Was the candle worth the cake?
Now you have it and you eat it
Does it make your belly ache?

*Hitting the bottle
and loosening
inhibitions, on the
Caribbean island
of Grenada.*

Photo: A. Vergani

CLICHÉS FOR AN UNFAITHFUL HUSBAND
by Jane King, Saint Lucia

– *Nawal El Saadawi* *on eternal love* –

*h*E SAID TO HER: I will love you forever.

She said: If you want me to believe you, do not say forever.

He said: You must believe that my love for you will last forever.

She said: I beg of you, do not say forever if you wish me to believe that what you say is true.

He said: But I swear to love you with a love which will remain eternally true.

She asked: What do you swear by when you say that your love for me will last forever?

I swear by God, my land and the Imam.

She said: Then I believe you and will put my life completely in your hands. My mind, my heart, my body, make me what I am and in love they are all one for you to have.

In the morning she saw his picture in the paper. It was a big picture and showed him wearing the Medal of Valour on Victory Day. Underneath was a short line announcing his marriage to the daughter of the Chief of Security.

She said: Yesterday you said to me that you love me.

He said: That was yesterday, but today is not the same day as it was yesterday.

She said: Can you betray me and yet remain faithful to your country?

He said: I am not one man. I am two men in one. The man who was with you yesterday is not the man I really am. He was the other man. I am the man who loves you dearly. Love and marriage are two different things and should not be seen as one.

She said: Then you married her without love.

He said: Her father was after me all the time, hunting me down like Satan, so I said to myself to avoid the harm he can do to me the best thing is for me to take the apple of his eye from him. Then he will fall right into my hand and be forced to do what I wish. I needed to possess her and where it is a question of possessing, to speak of love is no longer relevant.

The following night he found her lying in the arms of another man. When he saw the face of this other man he started to tremble all over, for the man was no other than the Chief of Security in person.

He said: Do you betray me with another man?

She said: I am not one woman. I am two women in one. The woman who was with you yesterday is not the woman I really am. She is the other woman. I am the woman who loves you, and who will love you for all time. Love and marriage are two different things and should not be looked upon as one.

He asked: Is he your husband?

She said: He kept threatening my father with imprisonment, so I said to myself to avoid the harm he can do to us the best thing is for me to marry him as soon as I can. Thus he will fall right into my hands and be at my beck and call. I needed to possess him and where it is a matter of possession, to speak of love becomes irrelevant.

They embraced one another for a long, long while. No one could see them in the silent night. No one could hear them make a silent vow, as they swore by God, by their land and the Imam that their love would last forever. And at the peak of their ecstasy he said to her that according to *Shariat* a man could have four wives at the same time, but in love he could only love one woman. So she asked him: Are you a member of Hizb Allah or a member of Hizb Al Shaitan? I am a member of both parties, he said. Can one be a member of both parties at one time? There is nothing in *Shariat* which prohibits a man from being a member of two parties. Since I believe that God exists and since I believe that Satan exists and since I fear both of them, in order to avoid the harm which can come to me from either of them I decided to join the two parties, said he.

In the quiet of the night he heard her say: You live in eternal fear. ◆

from ERNAL LOVE
by Nawal El Saadawi, Egypt

In crowded and chaotic Cairo it takes ingenuity to find a little rooftop privacy.

Photo: J. Horner

hIDDEN PLEASURE
of waiting for waiting,

consolation of silence,
hint of a caress,
outline of shyness
and excesses,
absence of absence.

Evening will flutter
its trembling flame in the corners,
and the light of this sun
with no shadows at noon
will sing in our words.
You will reach out your hands
toward old delusions,

I will touch the fresh rain
of your open gaze.

And it will be the end
of every ending
and the beginning
of every beginning.

*A wedding reception
in a small
Amazonian
settlement in North-
East Brazil.*

*Photo: M. Edwards/
Still Pictures*

HIDDEN PLEASURE
by Fanny Fierro, Ecuador

– Alifa Rifaat's gentle conspiracy –

ZEINAT WOKE to the strident call of the red cockerel from the rooftop above where she was sleeping. The Ghobashi house stood on the outskirts of the village and in front of it the fields stretched out to the river and the railway track.

The call of the red cockerel released answering calls from neighbouring rooftops. Then they were silenced by the voice of the *muezzin* from the lofty minaret among the mulberry trees calling: 'Prayer is better than sleep.'

She stretched out her arm to the pile of children sleeping alongside her and tucked the end of the old rag-woven *kilim* round their bodies, then shook her eldest daughter's shoulder.

'It's morning, another of the Lord's mornings. Get up, Ni'ma — today's market day.'

Ni'ma rolled onto her back and lazily stretched herself. Like someone alerted by the sudden slap of a gust of wind, Zeinat stared down at the body spread out before her. Ni'ma sat up and pulled her *galabia* over her thighs, rubbing at her sleep-heavy eyes in the rounded face with the prominent cheekbones.

'Are you going to be able to carry the grain to the market, daughter, or will it be too heavy for you?'

'Of course, mother. After all, who else is there to go?'

Zeinat rose to her feet and went out with sluggish steps to the courtyard, where she made her ablutions. Having finished the ritual prayer, she remained in the seated position as she counted off on her fingers her glorifications of Allah. Sensing that Ni'ma was standing behind her, she turned round to her:

'What are you standing there for? Why don't you go off and get the tea ready?'

Zeinat walked towards the corner where Ghobashi had stored the maize crop in sacks; he had left them as a provision for them after he had taken his air ticket from the office that had found him work in Libya and which would be bringing him back in a year's time.

'May the Lord keep you safe while you're away, Ghobashi,' she muttered.

Squatting in front of a sack, the grain measure between her thighs, she scooped up the grain with both hands till the measure was full, then poured it into a basket. Coughing, she waved away the dust that rose up to her face, then returned to her work.

The girl went to the large clay jar, removed the wooden covering and dipped the mug into it and sprinkled water on her face; she wetted the tips of her fingers and parted her plaits, then tied her handkerchief over her head. She turned to her mother:

'Isn't that enough, mother? What do we want the money for?'

Zeinat struck her knees with the palms of her hands and tossed her head back.

'Don't we have to pay off Hamdan's wage? — or was he cultivating the beans for us for nothing, just for the fun of hard work?'

Ni'ma turned away and brought the stove from the window shelf, arranging the dried corn-cobs in a pyramid and lighting them. She put it alongside her mother, then filled the teapot with water from the jar and thrust it into the embers. She squatted down and the two sat in silence. Suddenly Zeinat said:

'Since when has the buffalo been with young?'

'From after my father went away.'

'That's to say, right after the Great Feast, daughter?'

Ni'ma nodded her head in assent, then lowered it and began drawing lines in the dust.

'Why don't you go off and see how many eggs have been laid while the tea's getting ready.'

Zeinat gazed into the glow of the embers. She had a sense of peace as she stared into the dancing flames. Ghobashi had gone and left the whole load on her shoulders: the children, the two *kirats* of land and the buffalo. 'Take care of Ni'ma,' he had said the night before he left. 'The girl's body has ripened.' He had then spread out his palms and said: 'O Lord, for the sake of the Prophet's honour, let me bring back with me a marriage dress for her of pure silk.' She had said to him: 'May your words go straight from your lips to Heaven's gate, Ghobashi.' He wouldn't be returning before the following Great Feast. What would happen when he returned and found out the state of affairs? She put her head between →

The women of the family get together to bake bread in this oasis town of the Egyptian Sahara. Each household has its own cupola-shaped oven in the courtyard.

Photo: A. Vergani

the palms of her hands and leaned over the fire, blowing away the ashes. 'How strange,' she thought, 'are the girls of today! The cunning little thing was hanging out her towels at the time of her period every month just as though nothing had happened, and here she is in her fourth month and there's nothing showing.'

Ni'ma returned and untied the cloth from round the eggs, put two of them in the fire and the rest in a dish. She then brought two glasses and the tin of sugar and sat down next to her mother, who was still immersed in her thoughts.

'Didn't you try to find some way out?'

Ni'ma hunched her shoulders in a gesture of helplessness.

'Your father's been gone four months. Isn't there still time?'

'What's the use? If only the Lord were to spare you the trouble of me. Wouldn't it be for the best, mother, if my foot were to slip as I was filling the water jar from the canal and we'd be done with it?'

Zeinat struck herself on the breast and drew her daughter to her.

'Don't say such a wicked thing. Don't listen to such promptings of the Devil. Calm down and let's find some solution before your father returns.'

Zeinat poured out the tea. In silence she took quick sips at it, then put the glass in front of her and shelled the egg and bit into it.

Ni'ma sat watching her, her fingers held round the hot glass. From outside came the raised voices of women discussing the prospects at the day's market, while men exchanged greetings as they made their way to the fields. Amidst the voices could be heard Hamdan's laughter as he led the buffalo to the two *kirats* of land surrounding the house.

'His account is with Allah,' muttered Zeinat. 'He's fine and doesn't have a worry in the world.'

Ni'ma got up and began winding round the end of her headcloth so as to form a pad on her head. Zeinat turned round and saw her preparing herself to go off to the market. She pulled her by her *galabia* and the young girl sat down again. At this moment they heard knocking at the door and the voice of their neighbour, Umm al-Khair, calling:

'Good health to you, folk. Isn't Ni'ma coming with me to market as usual, Auntie Zeinat. Or isn't she up yet?'

'Sister, she's just going off to stay with our relatives.'

'May Allah bring her back safely.'

Ni'ma looked at her mother enquiringly, while Zeinat placed her finger to her mouth. When the sound of Umm al-Khair's footsteps died away, Ni'ma whispered:

'What are you intending to do, mother? What relatives are you talking about?'

Zeinat got up and rummaged in her clothes box and took out a handkerchief tied round some money, also old clothes. She placed the handkerchief in Ni'ma's palm and closed her fingers over it.

'Take it — they're my life savings.'

Ni'ma remained silent as her mother went on:

'Get together your clothes and go straight away to the station and take a ticket to Cairo. Cairo's a big place, daughter, where you'll find protection and a way to make a living till Allah brings you safely to your time. Then bring it back with you at dead of night without anyone seeing you or hearing you.'

Zeinat raised the end of her *galabia* and put it between her teeth. Taking hold of the old clothes, she began winding them round her waist. Then she let fall the *galabia*. Ni'ma regarded her in astonishment:

'And what will we say to my father?'

'It's no time for talking. Before you go off to the station, help me up with the basket so that I can go to the market for people to see me like this. Isn't it better, when he returns, for your father to find himself with a legitimate son than an illegitimate grandson?' ◆

The symbol painted on the wall of this Cairo house is meant to protect its inhabitants from misfortune.

Photo: A. Heitmann

from **AN INCIDENT IN THE GHOBASHI HOUSEHOLD**
by Alifa Rifaat, Egypt

– a moment of intense,
loving awareness
from Fahmida Riaz –

COME, GIVE ME YOUR HAND
touch my body
and listen to the beating of your child's heart
On that side of the navel
can you feel it stirring?

Leave it here
for a little while longer, this hand on my cold body
My restless being has found tranquility
My Jesus, the healer of my pain
every pore of my body
finds relief through this palm
Beneath this palm my precious child seems to turn.

Let your fingers know its body
get to know it
let me kiss these fingers of yours
let me kiss each and every fingertip
let me touch your nails with my lips
let me hide my face in this palm for a bit
these green fingers which bring flowers
With the tears which bubble up in my eyes
I shall tend these
the roots of these fingers which bring flowers
let me kiss them
the hair, the moon of your forehead, your lips
these shining black eyes,
so amazed at my trembling lips and my brimming eye.

What do you know? What do you know of
how you have transformed me?
Within me was a haunting darkness
a limitless, endless space
I wandered around aimlessly
longing for a taste of life
with tears filling my heart, I laughed at everyone
you filled my womb so
that light pours forth from my body.

All the sacred texts that ever descended
all the prophets sent to earth
all the angels beyond the clouds
colour, music, melody, flowers, buds and trees
at dawn the swaying branches of the trees
the meanings which were assigned to all of these
All the songs of joy which have been sung to earthly beings
all the saints, all the fakirs, all the prophets,
all the visionaries
the gods of well-being, beauty, goodness, God –
in all of them today
I have come to believe, I have come to believe.

COME, GIVE ME YOUR HAND
by Fahmida Riaz, Pakistan

love and life

In spite of the rise in fundamentalism, gender relations are changing in some communities in predominantly Muslim countries like Bangladesh and Pakistan. Voluntary groups are encouraging women to be less tied to the home and men to get more involved in childcare.

Photo: S. Alam/ Drik Picture Library

*– the pangs of maternal
and grandmaternal love
by Shashi Deshpande –*

I SMILE AS I HEAR THEM AT LAST, the sounds I am waiting for. A rush of footsteps, the slam of the bathroom door... I wince as the sound whams through the silent house... and, a minute later, another bang. And then, bare feet running towards me.

'You shouldn't bang the doors that way,' I say reproachfully. 'You might wake Mummy.'

She sits opposite me, cross-legged on the low wooden stool, hair tousled, cheeks flushed. 'Oh, she won't wake up for hours yet, she says cheerfully. 'Have you had your tea, *ajji*?' Our daily routine. I can never confess to her that I have had a cup an hour earlier. This is her joy, that I wait for her.

'No, I've been waiting for you. Have you brushed your teeth?'

She makes a face. 'I'll do it later,' she says, trying to be brusque and casual.

'You'll do no such thing. Go and brush them at once.'

'Only today, ajji. From tomorrow, I promise, I'll brush them first,' she cajoles.

'Nothing doing.' I try hard to be firm. But I can't fool her. She knows I am on her side. She lowers her voice to a conspiratorial whisper. 'Mummy won't know. She's sleeping.'

Now, of course, she leaves me no choice. I have to be firm. She goes reluctantly. And is back so fast, I have to ask, 'Did you really brush? Properly? Show me.'

'Look.'

I have to grin back at the grinning, impish face. 'Now tea for me.'

'No,' I say, 'tea for me. Milk for you.'

Ultimately, as always, we compromise and her tea is a pale brown. I switch off the Primus and, without the hissing sound, our voices sound loud and clear. We look at each other guiltily, thinking of the sleeper, and try to speak in lowered tones. Happiness can mean so many things to so many people. For me, it is this. The beginning of a new day with this child. We talk of so many things. But too soon it is time for her to go to school. Bathed and fresh, she sets off.

When when she is gone, silence settles on the house. A silence that will not lift till she returns. I had got used to this silence in the last seven years. It had never seemed terrible to me. It was a friendly silence, filled with the ghosts of so many voices in my life. They came back to keep me company when I was alone... my younger brother, my aunt who loved me when I was a child, my two infant sons who never grew up, and even the child Aarti, who seems to have no connection with this thin, bitter woman who now shares the silence with me. But since she came, the friendly ghosts have all gone.

It is late before she wakes. I have had my bath, finished my *puja*, and am half-way through cooking lunch, when I hear her stirring. I take down the *dal* from the fire and put on the tea. By the time tea is ready, she comes into the kitchen. Wordlessly she takes a cup from me. She drinks it in hungry gulps as if she has been thirsting for hours, then thrusts the cup back at me. I pour out some more. I, too, say nothing. Earlier, I used to ask, 'Slept well?' And one day, she had put down the cup with a trembling hand and said, 'Slept well? No, I never do that. I haven't slept well since Madhav died. I'll never sleep well again all my life. I have to take something every night so that I can close my eyes for a few hours. Now, never ask me again if I slept well.' Nine months I carried this daughter of mine in my body. I had felt within me every beat of her heart, every movement of her limbs. But... and this my doctor had told me then... my pains and shocks could never penetrate to her, she was so well protected. Even now, she is protected from my pains. Even now, I have no protection against her pains. I suffer with her, but like all my other emotions, it is a futile suffering. For I cannot help her. I can only fumble and blunder and make things worse. ◆

from **MY BELOVED CHARIOTEER**
by Shashi Deshpande, India

A Bhutanese grand-mother and her granddaughter mend clothes together. Living in an extended family – usual in the Indian sub-continent – encourages closer bonds across generations.

Photo: M. Brauen

MY MOTHER was very small
like mint or grass; she hardly cast a shadow
over things, hardly,
and the earth loved her
when it felt her lightness
and because she smiled upon it
in happiness and in pain.

Children loved her,
and the old ones, and the grass,
and the light that loves grace —
it searched for her and wooed her.

*An old woman's
open door in
Havana, Cuba.*

*Photo: B. Lewis/
Network*

from **MY MOTHER**
by Gabriela Mistral, Chile

I'LL KILL YOU.

Her voice said, soft and sweet by her lover's side. He smiled the smug smile of a man who knows he is loved. And anyway, she said it so gently that despite the strange shadowy glint in her eyes it sounded like a caress.

'I'll kill you if you leave me.'

This time her voice was more assured, as she stroked the man's hair and bare shoulders.

'So you want to force me to love you?'

'I hate you.'

'Why do you hug me then?'

'Because when I don't hate you, I love you.'

'You don't hate me.'

'I've told you, I'm crazy... if I weren't, how come I go on hugging you..?'

'That's not being crazy.'

'What is it then?'

'It means you're too hot-blooded, that's all.'

She kissed him. He smiled his almost female smile and said: 'Let's go to sleep; I have to get up early tomorrow.'

'You should find yourself a stone.'

'Why, am I a stone?'

'Yes.'

'What you said scared me.'

'What was that?'

'That you'd force me to marry you. It wouldn't do you any good. Even if you succeeded, I'd divorce you straightaway.'

'I know that from the last time, and I haven't forced you into anything.'

'But if you say it, it's because you're thinking it.'

'I don't want to force you to love me... I said it to see what you're made of.'

'What I'm made of? The same as ever. Why do you want to know what I'm made of?'

'Because I can't live with a man who abandons me when I'm pregnant. Last time you didn't come back until...'

'Tell me... are you pregnant now?'

'No.'

'Sure?'

'Sure.'

'Let's go to sleep.'

He turned his back to her.

'You used to sleep in my arms.'

He gave no reply. Realising how tired he was, she kept silent, feeling tenderness and pity for him. 'He's just a poor kid who won't accept any responsibility in life,' she thought as she fell asleep, not wanting to explore her thoughts any further.

As usual, she woke up late; she couldn't bear to watch the time go by, stretching out endlessly until he came back. She would wake up and lie in bed listlessly, filled with regrets. When she thought of her mother, the knot of emotion in her chest swelled until it took her over completely, choking her so she could scarcely breathe.

'How good mothers are!' she had said to him two nights earlier.

'Why's that?'

'I don't know... but they are good.'

'Maybe it's because they forgive us everything.'

'It could be.'

That was the frightful thing: mothers forgave everything, but that did not stop them suffering.

'Graciela, don't go with that man. If you do, you'll never set foot in this house again.'

She did go off with him, and when she came back her mother said not a word. She cooked her favourite dishes for her, scurried about for things to offer her. She looked after and spoilt her just like when she had been a child. That was the dreadful thing: she had forgiven her, but went on suffering. When the telegram arrived: 'If you have sorted everything out as you say, come back,' she ran after the man even though she was still weak. She had lost a lot of blood and the doctor had told her to rest. Her mother did not cry, pretended she knew nothing, but she did know. Her eyes seemed to be saying: 'What are you doing with a man who doesn't want your children?' →

Night falls over the Caribbean island of Dominica and love-lives play out under the tin roofs.

Photo: A. Vergani

They met; back in bed again, he begged her forgiveness, but by now there was nothing left to forgive. His repentance left her feeling sorry for him because he was a coward, because he was so selfish, such a tiny child, as small as an amoeba. She felt for him what mothers feel for their problem child: pity. She said 'my baby' to him, 'it's nothing, my baby'; every time she spoke to him she called him 'my baby'. But when she was all alone she knew she had not forgiven him, and that she felt two contradictory emotions for that man. They argued, they fought, and then said the sweetest things to each other; their bodies exchanged the softest caresses. But it was Hell. 'Today I'm finishing with him.' She would pack her bags, spend the whole afternoon folding and packing her clothes ready to leave; but then he knocked on the door, she opened it, they kissed, and she forgot everything, devouring him in bed, in his bed.

Someone knocked at the door. It was noon, time for the cleaner to come and do the room. The room... if only they lived in a house... then she could clean, could put up lace curtains and so perhaps no longer think about...

'May I clean the room, madam?'

The men who did the cleaning said 'madam' to her face, but behind her back called her the 'mistress' and uttered obscenities which made them laugh.

She went out to the balcony of the reception room. 'Why not throw myself from here?' The balcony was on the fifth floor, with a view of treetops, some terraced roofs and the long, white street lying there lifeless, steaming, unbearable. 'Why not throw myself from here?' She saw a boy ride past on a bicycle. What did she matter to that boy? What did she matter to anyone? She felt the same nausea she had been feeling for the past few days, the same nausea as the previous time. It made her eyelids droop so that the daylight became no more than a line where the treetops, the roofs, the lifeless street merged into one; simply a line of light. Inside her body, she could feel her blood and all her cells stirring as new streams flowed through her. 'What if I kept the child and fought for him?' The light grew more intense, more rounded. 'What if I were capable of digging in the earth with my bare hands to find him food... if I were capable... I'd take him through parks and streets to show him all the beauty that exists in things and people. All that I have never found for myself, but would be capable of finding through him and for him.'

When the lover returned, she had gone. ◆

from **A Man, a Woman**
by Omega Agüero, Cuba

IT'S A SERIES OF BALANCING ACTS – the world of work and leisure – if you are a woman. For the two urban friends in Ama Ata Aidoo's story it's about balancing the career with the man. How do you pursue your interests as a professional woman when your lover is deeply threatened by your success? For Domitila Barrios de **work and play** Chungara it's about growing up a girl in a tough Bolivian mining community. Social and economic changes can also make stability difficult, especially for rural Indian women who want to keep their customs but now go to work each day in an urban factory. For Jung Chang it's a case of trying to hold on to what matters for her as she endeavours to fit the mould of Mao's China – with some electrifying results!

*– Ama Ata Aidoo on what happens
to women who want a career –
and a man –*

M Y SISTER, if a man loves a woman, he would want to have her around as much as possible.'
'To the extent that he would want me to change my job because he thought it took me away from him?'
'Yes,' said Opokuya, wondering where she had acquired such ideas from, and the confidence to express them so forcefully. 'To the extent that he would want you to change your job.'
'But when we first met, Oko told me that what had attracted him most about me was my air of independence!'
Opokuya had begun to giggle, and then discovered she could hardly stop. 'You see, it happens to all of us. Esi, listen: men are not really interested in a woman's independence or her intelligence. The few who claim they like intelligent and active women are also interested in having such women permanently in their beds and in their kitchens.
'Which is impossible. It's a contradiction.'
'Yes. But there it is. Very few men realise that the sharp girls they meet and fall in love with are sharp because, among other things, they've got challenging jobs in stimulating places. That such jobs are also demanding. That these are also the kinds of jobs that keep the mind active – alive. Look, quite often, the first thing a man who married a woman mainly for the quickness of her brain tries to do is get her to change her job to a more "reasonable" one. Or to a part-time, not a full-time job. The pattern never, never changes. And then a "reasonable" job is often quite dull too.'
'And no part-time job has the stimulation that its full-time version can give.'
'Exactly! So that when a woman changes jobs in such a manner, more likely than not, her vision begins to shrink, and she begins to get bored and dissatisfied.'
'And even he might begin to find her dull.'
'Sure.'
Swiftly Esi had become aware of a certain desolation moving towards her from far away.
'It's an impossible situation,' she said rather heavily.
'It is,' Opokuya agreed, with equal cheerlessness. ◆

from **Changes**
by Ama Ata Aidoo, Ghana

Kenya's answer to the barefoot doctors, these health auxiliaries use motorbikes equipped with medical kits to reach distant villages where there is no healthcare. At first the village men frowned on the idea of women scooting around the countryside on motorbikes, but now it has become an accepted part of life.

Photo: C. Guarita/ Reportage

I LOVED SCHOOL. It was full of boys and girls. We played in the courtyard, gasping for breath as we ran from one end of it to the other, or sat splitting sunflower seeds between our teeth in rapid succession, or chewed gum with a loud smacking noise, or bought molasses sugar sticks and dry carob, or drank liquorice and tamarind and sugar cane juice; in other words, we went for everything with a deliciously strong flavour.

Once back I would sweep and clean the house, wash my uncle's clothes, make his bed and tidy his books. He bought me a heavy iron which I would heat on the kerosene stove, and use to launder his kaftan and turban. Shortly before sunset he would return from El Azhar. I served supper and we ate it together. The meal over, I lay on my sofa, while my uncle sat on his bed and read out aloud. I used to jump up to his side on the high bed, curl my fingers around his large hand with its long, thin fingers and touch his great big books, with their smooth, closely written pages, covered in fine black letters. I would try to make out a few words. They looked to me like mysterious signs that filled me with something like fear. El Azhar was an awesome world peopled only by men, and my uncle was one of them, was a man. When he read, his voice resonated with a sacred awe, and his great long fingers were seized with a strange trembling which I could feel under my hand. It was familiar, like a trembling experienced in childhood, a distant dream still remembered.

During the cold winter nights, I curled up in my uncle's arms like a baby in its womb. We drew warmth from our closeness. My face buried in his arms, I wanted to tell him that I loved him, but the words would not come. I wanted to cry but the tears would not flow. And after a while I would fall into a deep sleep until morning.

One day I fell sick with fever. My uncle sat on the bed by my side holding my head, patting my face gently with his great long fingers, and I slept all night holding on to his hand. ◆

A primary school in Egypt's Nile Valley, where almost as many girls as boys attend.

Photo: A. Vergani

from **WOMAN AT POINT ZERO**
by Nawal El Saadawi, Egypt

– Jung Chang joins the ranks in Mao's China –

BECOMING A WORKER was my only option. Most universities were still shut, and there were no other careers available. Being in a factory meant working only eight hours a day compared with the peasant's dawn-to-dusk day. There were no heavy loads to carry, and I could live with my family. But the most important thing was getting back my city registration, which meant guaranteed food and other basics from the state.

The factory was in the eastern suburbs of Chengdu, about forty-five minutes by bicycle from home. For much of the way I rode along the bank of the Silk River, then along muddy country roads through fields of rapeseed and wheat. Finally I reached a shabby-looking enclosure dotted with piles of bricks and rusting rolled steel. This was my factory. It was a rather primitive enterprise, with some machines dating back to the turn of the century. After five years of denunciation meetings, wall slogans, and physical battles between the factions in the factory, the managers and engineers had just been put back to work and it had begun to resume producing machine tools. The workers gave me a special welcome, largely on account of my parents: the destructiveness of the Cultural Revolution had made them hanker for the old administration, under which there had been order and stability.

I was assigned as an apprentice in the foundry, under a woman whom everyone called 'Auntie Wei'. She had been very poor as a child, and had not even had a decent pair of trousers when she was a teenager. Her life had changed when the Communists came, and she was immensely grateful to them. She joined the Party, and at the beginning of the Cultural Revolution she was among the Loyalists who defended the old Party officials. When Mao openly backed the Rebels, her group was beaten into surrender and she was tortured. A good friend of hers, an old worker who also owed much to the Communists, died after being hung horizontally by his wrists and ankles (a torture called 'duck swimming'). Auntie Wei told me the story of her life in tears, and said that her fate was tied to that of the Party, which she considered had been wrecked by 'anti-Party elements' like Lin Biao. She treated me like a daughter, primarily because I came from a Communist family. I felt uneasy

with her because I could not match her faith in the Party.

There were about thirty men and women doing the same job as me, ramming earth into molds. The incandescent, bubbling molten iron was lifted and poured into the molds, generating a mass of sparkling white-hot stars. The hoist over our workshop creaked so alarmingly that I was always worried it might drop the crucible of boiling liquid iron onto the people ramming away underneath.

My job as a caster was dirty and hard. I had swollen arms from pounding the earth into the molds, but I was in high spirits, as I naively believed that the Cultural Revolution was coming to an end. I threw myself into my work with an ardor that would have surprised the peasants in Deyang.

In spite of my newfound enthusiasm, I was relieved to hear after a month that I was going to be transferred. I could not have sustained ramming eight hours a day for long. Owing to the goodwill toward my parents, I was given several jobs to choose from – lathe operator, hoist operator, telephone operator, carpenter, or electrician. I dithered between the last two. I liked the idea of being able to create lovely wooden things, but decided that I did not have talented hands. As an electrician, I would have the glamour of being the only woman in the factory doing the job. There had been one woman in the electricians' team, but she was leaving for another post. She had always attracted great admiration. When she climbed to the top of the electrical poles people would stop to marvel. I struck up an immediate friendship with this woman, who told me something which made up my mind for me: electricians did not have to stand by a machine eight hours a day. They could stay in their quarters waiting to be called out on a job. That meant I would have time to myself to read.

I received five electric shocks in the first month. Like being a barefoot doctor, there was no formal training: the result of Mao's disdain for education. The six men in the team taught me patiently, but I started at an abysmally low level. I did not even know what a fuse was. The woman electrician gave me her copy of *The Electricians' Manual*, and I plunged into it, but still came out confusing electric current with voltage. In the end, I felt ashamed →

Workers eating in the Baotou Iron and Steel Plant, China. Steel production was at the forefront of Mao Zedong's drive to 'modernize' China through industrialization.

Photo: W. Imber

of wasting the other electricians' time, and tried to copy what they did without understanding much of the theory. I managed fairly well, and gradually was able to do some repairs on my own.

One day a worker reported a faulty switch on a power distribution board. I went to the back of the board to examine the wiring, and decided a screw must have come loose. Instead of switching off the electric supply first, I impetuously poked my mains-tester cum screwdriver at the screw. The back of the board was a net of wires, connections, and joints carrying 380 volts of power. Once inside this minefield, I had to push my screwdriver extremely carefully through a gap. I reached the screw, only to find it was not loose after all. By then my arm had started to shake slightly from being taut and nervous. I began to pull it back, holding my breath. Right at the very edge, just as I was about to relax, a series of colossal jolts shot through my right hand and down to my feet. I leaped in the air, and the screwdriver sprang out of my hand. It had touched a joint at the entrance to the power distribution network. I sagged onto the floor, thinking I could have been killed if the screwdriver had slipped a little earlier. I did not tell the other electricians, as I did not want them to feel they had to go on calls with me.

I got used to the shocks. No one else made a fuss about them, either. One old electrician told me that before 1949, when the factory was privately owned, he had had to use the back of his hand to test the current. It was only under the Communists that the factory was obliged to buy the electricians mains-testers.

There were two rooms in our quarters, and when they were not on a call, most of the electricians would play cards in the outer room while I read in the inner room. In Mao's China, failure to join the people around you was criticised as 'cutting oneself off from the masses', and at first I was nervous about going off on my own to read. I would put my book down as soon as one of the other electricians came inside, and would try to chat with him in a somewhat awkward manner. As a result they seldom came in. I was enormously relieved that they did not object to my eccentricity. Rather, they went out of their way not to disturb me. Because they were so nice to me I volunteered to do as many repairs as possible.

One young electrician in the team, Day, had been in a high school until the start of the Cultural Revolution, and was considered very well educated. He was a good calligrapher and played several musical instruments beautifully. I was very attracted to him, and in the mornings I would always find him leaning against the door to the electricians' quarters, waiting to greet me. I found myself doing a lot of calls with him. One early spring day, after finishing a maintenance job, we spent the lunch break leaning against a haystack at the back of the foundry, enjoying the first sunny day of the year. Sparrows were chirping over our heads, fighting for the grains left on the rice plants. The hay gave off an aroma of sunshine and earth. I was overjoyed to discover that Day shared my interest in classical Chinese poetry, and that we could compose poems to each other using the same rhyme sequence as ancient Chinese poets had done. In my generation, few people understood or liked classical poetry. We were very late back to work that afternoon, but there were no criticisms. The other electricians only gave us meaningful smiles.

Soon Day and I were counting the minutes during our days off from the factory, eager to be back together. We sought every opportunity to be near each other, to brush each other's fingers, to feel the excitement of being close, to smell the smell of each other, and to look for reasons to be hurt – or pleased – by each other's half-spoken words.

Then I began to hear gossip that Day was unworthy of me. The disapproval was partly caused by the fact that I was considered special. One of the reasons was that I was the only offspring of high officials in the factory, and indeed the only one most of the workers had ever come into contact with. There had been many stories about high officials' children being arrogant and spoiled. I apparently came as a nice surprise, and some workers seemed to feel that no one in the factory could possibly be worthy of me.

They held it against Day that his father had been a Kuomintang officer, and had been in a labor camp. The workers were convinced I had a bright future, and should not be 'dragged into misfortune' by being associated with Day. ➞

Actually, it was purely by chance that Day's father had become a Kuomintang officer. In 1937, he and two friends were on their way to Yan'an to join up with the Communists to fight the Japanese. They had almost reached Yan'an when they were stopped at a Kuomintang roadblock where the officers urged them to join the Kuomintang instead. While the two friends insisted on pressing on to Yan'an, Day's father settled for the Kuomintang, thinking it did not matter which Chinese army he joined, as long as it fought the Japanese. When the civil war restarted he and his two friends ended up on opposite sides. After 1949, he was sent to a labor camp, while his companions became high-ranking officers in the Communist army.

Because of this accident of history, Day was sniped at in the factory for not knowing his place by 'pestering' me, and even for being a social climber. I could see from his drained face and bitter smiles that he was stung by the snide gossip, but he said nothing to me. We had only hinted at our feelings in allusions in our poems. Now he stopped writing poems to me. The confidence with which he had begun our friendship disappeared, and he adopted a subdued and humbled manner toward me in private. In public, he tried to appease the people who disapproved of him by awkwardly trying to show them he really thought nothing of me. At times I felt that he behaved in such an undignified way that I could not help being irritated as well as saddened. Having been brought up in a privileged position, I did not realize that in China dignity was a luxury scarcely available to those who were not privileged. I did not appreciate Day's dilemma, and the fact that he could not show his love for me, for fear of ruining me. Gradually we became alienated.

During the four months of our acquaintance, the word 'love' had never been mentioned by either of us. I had even suppressed it in my mind. One could never let oneself go, because consideration of the vital factor, family background, was ingrained in one's mind. The consequences of being tied to the family of a 'class enemy' like Day's were too serious. Because of the subconscious self-censorship I never quite fell in love with Day. ◆

From **WILD SWANS**
by Jung Chang, China

*– how Domitila Barrios de Chungara
and her sisters were brought up
always to feel equal to boys –*

*i*T'S TRUE, MY FATHER was always concerned about our education. When my mother died, people would look at us and say: 'Oh, the poor little things, five women, not one man...what good are they? They'd be better off dead.' But my daddy would say proudly: 'No, let my girls alone, they're going to live.' And when people tried to make us feel bad because we were women and weren't much good for anything, he'd tell us that all women had the same rights as men. And he'd say that we could do the same things men do. He always raised us with those ideas. Yes, it was a very special discipline. And all that was very positive in terms of our future. So that's why we never considered ourselves useless women.

The teacher understood all that, because I told him about it. And we made a deal that I'd ask him for all the school supplies I needed. And from that day on we got on very well. And the teacher would give me and my little sisters all the supplies we needed. And that's how I was able to finish my last year in school, in 1952.

In school I learned to read, to write, and to get along. But I can't say that school really helped me to understand life. I think that education in Bolivia, despite the various reforms there have been, is still part of the capitalist system we live in. They always give an alienating education. For example, they make us see the motherland like a beautiful thing in the national anthem, in the colors of the flag, and all those things stop meaning anything when the motherland isn't well. The motherland, for me, is in every corner, it's also in the miners, in the peasants, in the people's poverty, their nakedness, their malnutrition, in their pains and their joys. That's the motherland, right? But in school they teach us to sing the national anthem, to parade, and they say that if we refuse to parade we aren't patriotic, and, nevertheless, they never explain our poverty, our misery, our parents' situation, their great sacrifices and their low wages, why a few children have everything and many others have nothing. They never explained that to me in school. ◆

from LET ME SPEAK
by Domitila Barrios de Chungara, Bolivia

Football is a passion for both sexes here in Llallagua, up in the Bolivian Andes. Most people live by mining here, the standard of living is low, the climate harsh and you have to be tough to survive.

Photo: A. Heitmann

– not much sleep
for Assumpta Acam-Oturu's
village woman –

WAKE UP WOMAN!
The Cock is crowing;
It's three a.m.
Wake up – it's time to weed the fields
in the distant hills.
Sleep no more;
Arise from the burdens of yesterday,
Forget the hours of toil
In that hot sun
That arose when you worked in the field
But set while you hurried to clear the weeds.
In the dark you return, as you left,
To those empty cooking pots.
Alas! the day is over
When the family enjoys the day's meal
But before you rest your feet
A voice calls: Woman get me hot water!
With that you know it's over
Until the cock crows
And the circle begins again:
Wake up woman!
Wake up woman!

ARISE TO THE DAY'S TOIL
by Assumpta Acam-Oturu, Uganda

  work and play

A Ugandan village woman prepares the daily meal. It's the rainy season so she has stacked the wood around her hut to stop it getting damp. Rural women in Africa still do most of the work – they grow and cook food, gather wood and water, and take charge of raising children.

Photo: G. Stark

*f*ROM THEN ON in my life, I remember everything. I played a lot with my younger sister when she was four and I was five. The ground would get hot in the middle of the day, and Sharifa and I would jump – aa-aa-aa-aa! We'd run to where the grass was – no shoes – and we'd rub our feet in the grass. The grass was rough. It pinched us, and aaaaah! When it rained, we'd bury our clothes in the ground to keep them dry, and we'd take a shower naked and run naked, and when the rain stopped we'd dig and get our clothes out. And shake them and wear them again! It was nice!

Sharifa was four years old and she was beautiful. One evening Mama was praying, and she ran to Mama and said, 'Mama, Mama, I'm cold, I'm cold'. Mama had a shawl around her shoulders, and she covered my sister with it and put her on her lap and rubbed her and said, 'What's wrong with you, Sharifa, what's wrong?' My sister said, 'Mama, I'm cold'. She wanted some milk, so Mama gave it to her. And then Sharifa started to moan, 'Unnnnh, unnnnnh,' and her fever got higher and she began to shiver and have chills. Since my father was a chief, we had some blankets, and my mother brought her inside and covered her up with them. But my sister began shaking all over and moaning louder – 'Unnh...unnh...unnh...' My father wasn't there. He and my mother were already divorced, and to walk from where we were staying in the interior to the town where he was took twenty-four hours. It would be a long way to carry a child as big as Sharifa. So my mama sent some men to look for Daddy, to tell him to come back and drive his daughter to the hospital in the city. Sharifa was sick for about four days. On the fourth day my daddy came, as the sun was going down, and soon after he came, she died. They buried her the next morning. And I remember being alone. ◆

from **AMAN. THE STORY OF A SOMALI GIRL**
by Aman, Somalia

Play is easy and work is looking after goats for nomadic children. These come from Niger.

*Photo: C. Beckwith/
Robert Estall
Picture Library*

SANGAREDDY WAS A VILLAGE fifty years ago when my mother was a young girl. It was a very small place then – there was no electricity; water was pulled out of deep wells and whatever happened in the village happened on Fridays, a day of Sabbath for the Muslims and market day for the peasants. They came in carts and met each other, bartered grain, gossiped: about the land, the harvest and their families. While fathers did business, children played, women bought things for the home. Each Friday the village met, affirming its patterns, its sense of itself.

Sangareddy was a village of paddy fields. A few farmers owned most of the land. Those who ploughed had no land. They received a share of the crop and a corner of the owner's roof that became a home. The man with the land was hailed as a giver. They called him *ayyaya* which in the Telugu language means 'father'. My grandfather, a Muslim patriarch, was *ayyaya* to all the dark rugged peasants who tilled his land and swore by Maissama, a local goddess, of whom my grandfather had no knowledge or understanding. His god and their goddess though had learnt to co-exist through the centuries. In a village essentially Hindu, my grandfather's was the only Muslim home. Scattered around its massive brick walls were the homes of peasants with walls of mud, roofs of grass and a tenor of life that had not changed for a long time. While my grandfather sat in the verandah, and delved into his books, my grandmother was out in the fields, watching the peasants at work, sharing their woes, their lives. My mother stayed in her room and learnt of the village from her mother. And, at night, while she counted stars through her window, she heard the cries, the laughter, the quarrels of men and women that broke through frail mud walls and reached her.

With the village she, too, waited to celebrate the turn of the seasons. When there was no rain, the peasants would come singing on the dusty paths carrying a huge basket on a wooden pole. There would be a large bull frog in the basket (that was padded with fresh neem leaves). The cry of *Hassana Hossana Uyalo* would fill the air. It was not a local ditty but an invocation to the memory of

Hasan and Hosain, grandsons of Prophet Mohammed, who signify for the Muslims martyrdom in the name of Islam and, for the peasants of Sangareddy, the power of miracles. When the frog in the basket would arrive at a home, the children would run out and pour pitchers of water on the frog. And lo! by the evening, the clouds would roll, the heavens thunder and there would be rain.

And at the time of harvest, when the women winnowed the wheat and the husk blew like yellow smoke in the wind, it would be time for *kanduru*, a feast to mark the season of ripening, the readying of the crop. Lambs would be bought and slaughtered, food cooked and a Muslim priest invited to bless the offerings with a *fateha*, a prayer from the Koran. The prayer mattered, not the language in which it was recited. Food brought rejoicing, a celebration diffused barriers of caste, religion, riches and poverty.

Even today Pochamma swears by my dead grandmother who shared her feast and blessed each child that she delivered. When I ask her how many children she brought into this world, she quips: 'Do you question when the land ripens? Why, then, do you worry if a woman comes of age and bears life? It is the nature of women to bear children as it is the nature of the land to bear fruit and flower.'

For women in the village children happened naturally, remembers my mother. 'I would see a woman one day with a bulging belly. In a few days she would be back in the field with a babe in a sack tied to a tree. The Banjara women who wandered through villages, and broke stones on the high road, would just spread out their wide mirror skirts and deliver babies. There was not even a village *dai* available to them. Children died as naturally as they were born. When a child came, they rejoiced without ceremony. And, when it died, there was no mourning. To celebrate a joy or dwell on a pain, takes time, money and food.'

'The walls have shrunk,' says my mother, who returned to see her house after half a century. The wide acres of paddy, that belonged to her father, are now patches of green owned by small farmers. The large tank, from where the village drew its drinking water, →

An Indian village woman carries out her routine daily tasks. But industrialization is reaching rural areas and rapidly changing lifestyles there.

Photo: A.Gatha

is mossy with violet hyacinth. Water now gushes out of bore wells where women no longer linger to gossip. Pochamma's son continues to till the field but her two daughters have begun to work in a factory that looms on the edge of the village. Even the Banjara women have disappeared. Or, perhaps, they have stopped wearing the wide mirror skirts that took them a year to stitch and craft. They have taken to the sari and have begun to look like the less rugged village women. Quiet continues to brood in the village, as it does in all the villages of India. It is no longer stoic, though. And it does not take a night in a slow bullock cart to reach. A pilgrimage for which my mother waited fifty years is now over in less than three hours. ◆

from UNVEILING INDIA
by Anees Jung, India

JESUS CHRIST MEETS BUDDHA meets Mohammed meets a Voodoo priestess meets the film star goddesses of the Hindi movie. There's Isabel Allende's Consuelo, lover of fictions, sacred and otherwise. And a mesmerizing mix of traditional and pop cultures from Gita Mehta. The divisions between the normal and the para- *culture and* normal can become blurred mingling the stuff of religion, *creativity* dreams and creative imaginings that create a culture. A traditional culture can be a terrible constraint, but also a vivid personal flag of identity especially for the 'fat black lady' living the Guyanese immigrant's life in the grey and dreary North but dreaming of 'a tropical death. Yes!'

*– the girl's religious reveries
aren't entirely sacred
in Isabel Allende's story –*

CONSUELO'S APPEARANCE set her apart from the others, and the nuns, sure that this was not accidental but a sign of benevolent divine will, spared no effort in cultivating her faith, in the hope she would decide to take her vows and serve the Church; all their efforts, however, came to naught before the girl's instinctive rejection. She made the attempt in good faith, but never succeeded in accepting the tyrannical god the nuns preached to her about; she preferred a more joyful, maternal, and compassionate god.

'That is the Most Holy Virgin Mary,' the nuns explained to her.

'She is God?'

'No, she is the Mother of God.'

'Yes, but who has the say in heaven, God or his Mama?'

'Quiet, silly girl. Be quiet and pray. Ask the Lord to give you light,' they counseled.

Consuelo would sit in the chapel and stare at the altar dominated by a terrifyingly realistic Christ and try to recite the rosary, but soon she would be lost in endless adventures in which her memories of the jungle alternated with the figures of Sacred History, each with his bundle of passions, vengeance, martyrdom, and miracles. She soaked it in greedily, all of it: the ritual words of the Mass, the Sunday sermons, the pious readings, the night noises, the wind in the colonnades, the witless expressions of the saints and anchorites in the niches of the church. She learned to hold her tongue, and prudently suppressed the treasure of her prodigious flow of fables until I gave her the opportunity to unloose the torrent of words stored within her.

Consuelo spent so much time in the chapel – motionless, hands clasped, placid as a cow chewing her cud – that the rumour spread through the convent that she was blessed with heavenly visions.

The Mother Superior, however, a practical Catalan woman less inclined than the other nuns of the congregation to believe in miracles, realized that Consuelo was touched not by saintliness but by an incurable bent for daydreaming. As the girl did not, in addition, show any enthusiasm for stitching mattresses, making the hosts for Mass, or weaving baskets, she judged her training to be complete, and placed her in the house of a foreign doctor named Professor Jones. She herself led Consuelo by the hand to a somewhat run-down but still splendid French-style mansion on the outskirts of the city, sitting at the foot of a hill authorities have now designated as a National Park. Consuelo's first impression of the doctor was so intense that it was months before she lost her fear of him. He came into the large parlor wearing a butcher's apron and carrying a strange metallic instrument. He was so preoccupied in his project that he did not even say hello; he dispatched the nun with four incomprehensible sentences and, with a grunt, packed Consuelo off to the kitchen. She, on the other hand, studied him in detail; she had never seen such a threatening individual. But she also noticed that he was as handsome as a picture of Jesus, all gold, with the same blond beard as the Prince of Peace, and eyes of an impossible colour. ◆

from EVA LUNA
by Isabel Allende, Chile

Although Protestant evangelism is on the rise, Roman Catholicism is still very much part of daily life in Latin America. This facade of Iglesia de San Andres Xecul, Totonicapan in the north-western highlands of Guatemala is repainted every year in different colours, the church's appearance altering according to the rhythm of village life.

Photo: J. Nelson

– Bessie Head's
fascination with the travels
of an old black pot –

IN EVERY HOMESTEAD in rural Botswana and indeed in many homes in Southern Africa, there is a remarkable cooking pot – the tripod, made entirely of iron with a round belly and resting on the ground on three stands or legs. The pot is of all sizes. For everyday household meals a small wood fire is lit directly under a medium size pot and it is as though the pot itself is a small portable cooking stove producing endless meals of boiled meat and porridge. For wedding feasts and funerals where large numbers of people have to be fed, immense versions of the iron pot are brought out and great log fires are lit under the pot to cook the enormous meals.

A cooking pot may seem a mundane and impossible subject to discuss but I am fascinated by history, by the migrations of people, by the meeting of many strange cultures and by trade and the exchange of goods. I had always associated the tripod, the open outdoor fireplace and its simple humility, with the lives of black people. It never occurred to me that the cooking pot was an imported item and had at some stage in history travelled thousands of miles over oceans to become an indispensable part of African homesteads.

Trade can change a whole way of life. At one stage it was necessary for me to attempt to reconstruct the self-sufficient traditional African society where people had produced all their own household goods. It was a difficult task as few of the traditional items have survived. The clay pots were fragile and so were the knives, axes and spears. They were rapidly discarded in favour of European goods. I interviewed an old woman who was one of the last clay-pot makers in the village. The skill of being a clay-pot maker had been transmitted to her by her mother but she had no daughter or granddaughter who was interested in learning the skill.

A hundred years ago, being a housewife in traditional African society was a highly skilled occupation. Women had to know how to produce many household items like clay pots and baskets for storing grain; they also had to plough the fields and produce the year's supply of corn, thatch and build the walls of mud huts. Today women simply buy sturdy galvanised iron buckets and other household items from the shops. But the old clay-pot maker told me: 'In the old days my clay pots were not only used to draw water. They were cooking pots as well.' I remember being astonished that such a fragile item as a clay pot, worked at patiently by hand and fired roughly over a home-made kiln, could be used for cooking. The interview also created a nagging worry in my mind. If clay pots had been cooking pots in the old days, where did the tripod come from? The tripods seemed such a traditional African household item that I failed to press the old people about their origins.

The answer to my worry came in a surprising way. I took a trip to Denmark and one evening I was taken out to a restaurant in Copenhagen for a meal. The restaurant was done up in the decor of an old-style Danish farmhouse. My hostess said to me: 'Our ancestors used an open hearth for cooking and an iron pot hung down by a chain from the chimney.'

The iron pot was missing from the decor but she quickly drew a sketch of it. It was the tripod that had travelled so far from its original home, Europe, and found another home on the African continent. Its usefulness as a cooking pot may be over in Europe but it is still very much alive on thousands of African hearths. ◆

from **THE OLD IRON COOKING POT OF EUROPE**
by Bessie Head, Botswana

Ndebele people of South Africa cook up a 'wedding soup' in a typical old iron pot. The 'bride price' – the gift the prospective groom has to make to the bride's family – is negotiated and then there is a party thrown by her parents to celebrate the engagement.

Photo: M. Courtney-Clark

*– Anita Desai's young
hero gets seduced
by the cinema –*

*t*HEN, WHEN I WAS OLDER, there was a time when only the cinema mattered. I saw four, five, as many as six cinema shows a week, creeping out of my room at night barefoot, for silence, with money stolen from my father, or mother, or anyone, clutched in my hand, then racing through the night-wild bazaar in time for the last show. Meena Kumari and Nargis were to me the queens of heaven, I put myself in the place of their screen lovers and felt myself grow great, hirsute, active and aggressive as I sat on the straw-stuffed seat, my feet tucked up under me, a cone of salted gram in my hand, uneaten, as I stared at these glistening, sequined queens with my mouth open. Their attractions, their graces filled up the empty spaces of my life and gave it new colours, new rhythms. So then I became aware of the women of our *mohalla* as women: ripe matrons who stood in their doorways, hands on hips, in that hour of the afternoon when life paused and presented possibilities before evening duties choked them off, and the younger girls, always moving, never still, eluding touch. They were like reeds in dirty water for however shabby they were, however unlike the screen heroines, they never quite lacked the enticements of subtle smiles, sly glances and bits of gold braid and lace. Some answered the look in my eyes, promised me what I wanted, later perhaps, after the late show, not now. ◆

Cinema is a vibrant part of modern popular Indian culture – and of the country's economy. India is the single biggest film producer in the world.

Photo: P. Frey

from **THE ACCOMPANIST**
by Anita Desai, India

– *a step into the supernatural for Clarice Lispector's Macabéa* –

S IT VERY DEAR?

'I'll loan you the money. Madame Carlota has the power to break any spells that might be worrying her clients. She broke mine on the stroke of midnight on Friday the thirteenth of August over at San Miguel, on a pitch where they practise voodoo. They bled a black pig and seven white hens over me and tore my bloodstained clothes to shreds. Can you pluck up enough courage?'

'I don't know if I could stomach all that blood.'

Perhaps because blood is everyone's secret, that life-giving tragedy. But Macabéa only knew that she could not stomach the sight of blood, the other reflections were mine. I am becoming interested in facts: facts are solid stones. There is no means of avoiding them. Facts are words expressed throughout the world.

Well then.

Faced with this sudden offer of help, Macabéa, who never remembered to ask for anything, asked her boss for time off by pretending she had toothache. She accepted a loan from Glória without having the faintest idea when she would be able to pay her back. This bold decision surprisingly encouraged her to make an even bolder decision (bang): since the money was on loan, she reasoned somewhat perversely, and was not strictly hers, then she was free to spend it. So for the first time in her life she took a taxi and asked to be dropped in Olaria. I suspect that she acted so boldly out of sheer desperation, even though she didn't know that she was desperate. She was at the end of her tether and felt completely worn out.

Tracing Madame Carlota's address turned out to be straightforward: so very straightforward that Macabéa thought of it as being a favourable omen. Madame Carlota's ground-floor apartment was situated on the corner of a cul-de-sac. On the pavement tiny blades of grass sprouted between the flagstones – Macabéa noticed them because she always noticed things that were tiny and insignificant. She thought dreamily, as she rang the doorbell: grass is so easy and simple. Her thoughts were gratuitous and unconnected because, however erratic, she possessed vast reserves of inner freedom.

It was Madame Carlota herself who came to the door. She greeted Macabéa amiably and said:

'My guiding spirit has already informed me of your visit, my dear. What is your name again? Ah, yes! A very pretty name. Come in, my pet. There is a client with me in the other room. If you don't mind waiting in here. Would you care for a coffee, my pet?'

Macabéa was taken aback, never having received so many endearments from anyone. ◆

from THE HOUR OF THE STAR
by Clarice Lispector, Brazil

This woman is a priestess of the Candomblé religion in Brazil, which derives from the Yoruba culture of Nigeria, Benin and Angola. Brought to Brazil by African slaves, much of the religion remains intact – particularly in the North East of the country.

Photo: B. Bosshart

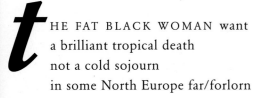

*t*HE FAT BLACK WOMAN want
a brilliant tropical death
not a cold sojourn
in some North Europe far/forlorn

The fat black woman want
some heat/hibiscus at her feet
blue sea dress
to wrap her neat

The fat black woman want
some bawl
no quiet jerk tear wiping
a polite hearse withdrawal

The fat black woman want
all her dead rights
first night
third night
nine night
all the sleepless droning
red-eyed wake nights

In the heart
of her mother's sweetbreast
In the shade
of the sun leaf's cool bless
In the bloom
of her people's bloodrest

the fat black woman want
a brilliant tropical death yes

A TROPICAL DEATH
by Grace Nichols, Guyana

  culture and creativity

Carnival time in Recife, Brazil. A blaze of crazy and colourful costumes fills the streets for five days and nights before Lent. In this country of great social divisions, daily roles are abandoned and everyone enters a world of make-believe.

Photo: P. Frey

*t*HE TROUBLE WITH MIRACLES is that confusion prevents discrimination. Difficulty is encountered in separating the chaff from the gross. One school of archeologists traces the origins of Christianity to exactly this confusion.

They believe that Jesus Christ during his absence from the Bible between the ages of twelve and thirty, was in fact traveling in India. In India Jesus found a guru who taught him much about mysticism, fasting and levitation. The archeologists argue that these sixteen years of training enabled Christ to spend forty days in the wilderness without food or drink. Also, through yogic control, Christ was able to remain in the tomb for three days and nights after his crucifixion. And finally, because of the meditations he did in the tomb during his incarceration, it was a simple matter for him to levitate on Easter Sunday, a feat not really worthy of the hallelujahs with which it has been commemorated for almost two thousand years.

The archeologists are convinced that Jesus levitated his way back to India, and spent the last years of his life in the Himalayas, where he achieved *moksha*, release from the cycle of life and death, and then allowed his body to die. His followers did not burn the body but buried it, so that the place could become a place of pilgrimage as befitted the tomb of a Master who had passed beyond Karma, and because he was a Jew they built for him a tomb in the Jewish mode. The archeologists are now fanning through the mountains around the Vale of Kashmir looking for this Jewish tomb. They have forgotten, as scientists sometimes will, that the hallelujahs were sung because good has triumphed over evil, not because the body had defeated death. ◆

from **KARMA COLA**
by Gita Mehta, India

Deities from many religions rub shoulders with muscle pumpers and local film stars on this poster stall in Trivandrum, South India.

Photo: B. Bosshart

– the thrill of change
from Malak'Abd al-Aziz –

W HEN WE ENTERED THE BAZAARS
We saw the veils of rose, of green...
And heard the prattle of the parrots,
Babbling every place.
The same empty words,
Smeared with oil and sweets
So that the artificial taste was concealed
and we proceeded with attentiveness.

At times, I had to dress for the circus, masked...
We'd stride above the tightrope – alone
And twist over the raised poles
We change colours like a banded chameleon
Which we overcame – and fell upon the truth
Like the sharpened edge of a sword
And we tumbled from above the tightrope,
From the highness of the top, the vertical height...

Our platform raises, grows higher, higher
Rises higher and rises above the tentpoles, it springs
And with the touch of a hand
We bared the veils – we unveiled the secret,
And we stood still in the nakedness of the birth of
purity and innocence...
We gleam, we radiate – beneath the sun
in the nakedness of truth.

THE FALL
by Malak'Abd al-Aziz, Egypt
Translated from the Arabic by Pamela Vittorio

  culture and creativity

*To veil or not to veil.
Such contrasts are
not uncommon in
Marrakesh. The
Moroccan city lies
halfway between the
strict Arab and
Islamic codes of the
veil in the North and
the relaxed attitudes
of the Berbers in the
South. But other
influences also figure
– working abroad
and prolonged
contact with Western
culture, for example.*

*Photo: B. Barbey/
Magnum*

– life, death and
nightmare-eating tapirs
by O Chonghui –

HIS WIFE'S OUTLINE was clearly visible through the open door. Drifting in and out of sleep, he saw her hands roll dough into the shape of a body with ears and horns and a tail and legs. It was a queer shape he had never seen before. Standing it in line with the other figures at the sunny edge of the veranda, she began muttering to herself: 'Grandfather suffered from nightmares till the day he died, and he had these splitting headaches. He himself didn't know whether the headaches came from the nightmares, or the other way around. We asked a shaman to do an exorcism and we had a blind man chant a Buddhist scripture, but those awful headaches just wouldn't go away...' By now he had heard the story of her grandfather, a well-known master carpenter, several times. 'He'd wake up screaming from an awful dream – late at night, early in the morning, whenever – and then roam the house like a madman because of a headache. Grandmother used to say he'd built too many houses where graves once were...' Ahead of him, at an indistinct bend in the corridor, he sees a screaming old man with an arched back and a white headband. 'That's why Grandfather carved those strange animals with his pocket knife. They looked like elephants or bears; whatever they were, they sure looked strange. Tapirs, I think he called them, and he said they ate nightmares .....' His wife continued to form shapes from the dough in the basin. 'Grandfather left them at his bedside next to the spittoon. And so he figured that what he had coughed up into the spittoon was actually the nightmares – the ones the tapirs had eaten all night long and thrown up first thing in the morning. His dying wish was to have the tapirs with him in his coffin. I guess he thought he'd have nightmares even after he died. Do dead people have dreams, too? I was a little girl then, and it was all very strange to me, but now I can understand why Grandfather did that. Back in the old days didn't people make mud figures of their belongings – and their servants, too – and ask to be buried with them?...' His wife's grandfather was sleeping comfortably now at the end of the long, faint corridor of time, the tapirs at his side.

As if mesmerised by his wife's slow, low-pitched chanting, he walked on through time, which was part buried in oblivion and part risen dimly before him. It was just like film applied unevenly with sensitizer: part of it clearly defined, almost luminous; part of it obscured, too dark. But he was not all that impatient to remember. Recalling only the things he wants to recall is the insignificant privilege of an old man. But what was this place where he hesitated to stop? An exhibition room in a museum he had once visited?

It was the room where clay figures, bronze mirrors, and other burial artifacts were displayed. When he saw the mirrors, cleansed of tarnish after thousands of years in the earth, he felt he had died long ago. All alone, he couldn't hear even his footsteps on the thick carpet. That was the reason, he told himself, for the mysterious, fleeting sentiment he experienced on his way out the long, dampish corridor. ◆

from **THE BRONZE MIRROR**
by O Chonghui, Korea

A candle-lit procession at a Buddhist temple just outside Seoul in South Korea. In spite of expanding industrialization Koreans are strong believers in Buddhism.

Photo: T. Tsukada

– panic in the household!
Bulbul Sharma's heroine finds herself
at the centre of a cosmic confusion –

*a*LL IT MEANT, the priest explained, not to me but to my mother, was that the planets had not been moving in their proper order when I was born and my husband would die before me. I saw nothing terrible in this but my mother and my grandmother set up a wailing at once and even the maids joined in. Though the women had always known this is what *mangalik* meant it was only when the priest pulled out his tattered red almanac and read out the exact time and date of my impending misfortune, that everything suddenly became official and my mother had to do something to mark the event. So she began beating her chest gently and crying.

After that was over, my father took charge. He called the priest into his study and shut the door on our curious faces like he always did when he entered that secret, forbidden room. As usual the women rushed to the window and sat down on the mat which was always kept there for them so that they could eavesdrop in comfort. The men began talking. The priest, an awkward young man, overcome by the honour of being allowed into the Raibahadur's special room, started stuttering and mumbling softly. We strained our ears to catch his words and my grandmother, who was slightly deaf, muttered angrily under her breath but did not dare curse him like she did when we mumbled. My father spoke loudly and clearly for our benefit because he hated repeating anything and he also wanted to finish the priest and my mother in one breath. 'I am not a superstitious man as you know,' he said looking at his bookshelf lined with heavy English journals and the priest too followed his gaze, muttering his ready agreement. 'I do not believe in all this nonsense but what has to be done has to be done. I have read the scriptures from beginning to end and all the ancient sages say the same thing. The *mangal grah* must be averted or else doom is certain.'

The priest coughed once or twice to say that he too shared the same thoughts. 'It is written that a girl who is a *mangalik* is cursed to become a widow even after marrying a *mangalik* boy, but another book says that there is a way to escape this.'

Now the priest suddenly spoke up loudly. 'I know... I know...

marry her to a peepal tree.'

My father did not like the way this important information was stolen from him and sat in stony silence for a while. The priest realised he had overstepped his brief and hung his head apologetically, in silence.

After a suitable pause to show his annoyance, my father began once more. 'The girl is to be married to a peepal tree and then widowed. In this way the planets are fooled and the curse is averted.'

The priest wanted to add many details to this curt information but he restrained himself. I could see him nodding his head and gulping down his rush of words.

'See to the arrangements and fix a date,' said my father and went back to studying the new English journal which had just come for him from England that morning. The priest stumbled out of the room and was immediately engulfed by the women in a warm, eager, questioning circle. 'What shall we do? You must tell us, Panditji. But first you must eat something,' said my mother and guided him to our sitting room. The priest, regaining his dignity and importance quickly under my mother's kindly gaze, started talking clearly and confidently once again. In fact he began sounding a lot like my father.

'You will make arrangements for the wedding as soon as possible. All the rituals should be carried out properly, especially the widowhood otherwise the gods will not believe it has happened,' he said, taking a small sip of the almond-flavoured milk my mother had placed before him. I will fix a date for the wedding after consulting the almanac. We will go to the riverside for the ceremony since the wedding and the widowing ceremonies can be performed there easily.'

'Whatever you say, Panditji. Just rid my daughter of this *grah*,' said my mother with a deep, sorrowful sigh which, after years of practice, she had become very good at.

'Yes... yes. Do not worry,' the priest replied, also looking solemn. But a tiny moustache of white foam covered his upper lip giving him the face of a sad clown and I could not help laughing. My →

The jewels worn by this woman from Rajasthan are not merely for ornamentation – they are good luck charms given to her during marriage. India is one of the few countries in the world where men outlive women – and there remains, among traditional families, a stigma against women who outlive their husbands.

Photo: D. Amsler

mother slapped me gently like she does to show outsiders how strict she is with me and folded her hands in apology to the priest. After reluctantly accepting a small box of sweets and casting a quick look at the closed door of my father's study, the priest left. My mother and I at once broke into loud laughter but were quickly silenced by a gentle cough from the study.

From the next day my mother began preparing for my mock wedding. She ordered the *munshi* to buy bales of red silk, sequins and English satins and our old tailor was told to move into the small room along the verandah. I was measured a hundred times a day as my mother made the old man open the stitches and remake every garment. 'Make it at least four inches bigger and then fold it. She can wear the same clothes for her real wedding. Why waste cloth?' she said, suddenly turning thrifty. But I was to have four new sets of gold ornaments though my mother had already made plenty of jewellery for me. She would often make me try on the glittering jewels and we both had a lot of fun doing this.

'This is a good time to get money out of your father. He will give readily now so why miss the chance?' she said, her eyes full of love and greed for me.

A dozen red and green glass bangles were bought too and my mother, for the first time, especially asked for the cheap thin ones. 'They have to be broken. The expensive ones will take a long time and your father is sure to get angry.' She also bought one cheap white sari for me to wear when I was widowed but for some reason she kept it bundled up in one corner and would not let me look at it. She kept ordering little things like silver boxes for *sindoor*, *mehndi*, red ribbons, and gold buttons every day and the poor *munshi* rushed in and out of the house with her lists.

Everyone in the house was infected by my mother's enthusiasm and her frantic preparations and even my father stopped by on his way out one day to see what the tailor was doing and made him spoil an entire row of stitches! Only my brother kept muttering that all this was a load of rubbish and we were behaving like illiterate people, but since he never had the courage to protest in front of my father, the only literate person beside him, we did not care what he thought of us or my impending wedding. ◆

from **RITES OF PASSAGE**
by Bulbul Sharma, India

      culture and creativity

NOISY, CROWDED HOUSES and all the bustle and chaos of megacity life. Vast arid pastures in which a nomadic woman gives birth. This is the real environment for women – not the conventional, male, romantic view of nature. And the sniff of the real is powerful in the writings of Somalia's Aman or India's Anita Desai. *environment* For the Andean Indians in Luisa Valenzuela's story the connection with nature goes, quite literally, without saying. While the cliché about women being 'closer to nature' is given an ironic twist by the fact that women are often the first to suffer when the environment is damaged – thanks usually to decisions made by men.

— environmental bombardment —
of the domestic kind —
for Anita Desai's student —

tURN IT OFF, TURN IT OFF, turn it off! First he listens to the news in Hindi. Directly after, in English. Broom — brroom — brrroom — the voice of doom roars. Next, in Tamil. Then in Punjabi. In Gujarati. What next, my god, what next? Turn it off before I smash it onto his head, fling it out of the window, do nothing of the sort of course, nothing of the sort.

— And my mother. She cuts and fries, cuts and fries. All day I hear her chopping and slicing and the pan of oil hissing. What all does she find to fry and feed us on, for God's sake? Eggplants, potatoes, spinach, shoe soles, newspapers, finally she'll slice me and feed me to my brothers and sisters. Ah, now she's turned on the tap. Its roaring and pouring, pouring and roaring into a bucket without a bottom.

— The bell rings. Voices clash, clatter and break. The tin-and-bottle man? The neighbours? The police? The Help-the-Blind man? Thieves and burglars? All of them, all of them, ten or twenty or a hundred of them, marching up the stairs, hammering at the door, breaking in and climbing over me — ten, twenty or a hundred of them.

— Then, worst of all, the milk arrives. In the tallest glass in the house. 'Suno, drink your milk. Good for you, Suno. You need it. Now, before the exams. Must have it. Suno. Drink.' The voice wheedles its way into my ear like a worm. I shudder. The table tips over. The milk runs. The tumbler clangs on the floor. 'Suno, Suno, how will you do your exams?'

— That is precisely what I ask myself. All very well to give me a room — Uncle's been pushed off on a pilgrimage to Hardwar to clear a room for me — and to bring me milk and say, 'Study, Suno, study for your exam.' What about the uproar around me? These people don't know the meaning of the word Quiet. When my mother fills buckets, sloshes the kitchen floor, fries and sizzles things in the pan, she thinks she is being Quiet. The children have never even heard the word, it amazes and puzzles them. On their way back from school they fling their satchels in at my door, then tear in to snatch them back before I tear them to bits. Bawl when I pull their ears, screech when mother whacks them. Stuff themselves with her fries and then smear the grease on my books. ◆

from **STUDIES IN THE PARK**
by Anita Desai, India

Privacy is a luxury that only the richest of Indians can afford — and this family have few secrets from passers-by in their Bombay Street. Even middle-class Indian families are accustomed to living in noisy and cramped domestic conditions with several generations sharing a house.

Photo: R. Singh

– life –
and the land of dreams –
by Amina Saïd –

ᴀ ND WE WERE BORN
without the slightest choice of worlds

the wind gathers
our solitudes
leaves branches trees
our bodies strangers to eternity

there is a land in us
which feeds our dreams
from within

just as the night
secretly
feeds the night
by an intuition of the world
we sensed the blind
shore
the unforeseeable place

what are we going to
begin anew?

ᴀɴᴅ Wᴇ ᴡᴇʀᴇ Bᴏʀɴ
by Amina Saïd, Tunisia

78   *environment*

Mainly women and children live in this Berber village of Chenini in the extreme south of Tunisia. Their menfolk are away, working in the cities or abroad, and the women are left to support their families. One of their major tasks is searching for firewood, which proves increasingly difficult in a part of the world where the desert creeps nearer day by day.

Photo: A-M. Grobet

– an Andean fantasy
from Luisa Valenzuela –

You're going to find it hard to believe what I tell you because these days who knows anything about life in the country? And up there, life on the mountain, up among the eagles? But you get used to it. Oh, yes. I can say that, I who never knew anything but the city, see how I am now, the colour of earth, carrying my pails of water from the public fountain. Water for myself and water for others. I do it to eke out a living; I've done it ever since the day I made the foolish mistake of climbing the path that borders the cliff. I climbed up, and when I looked down and saw the green dot of the valley far below, I decided to stay here forever. It wasn't that I was afraid, I was just being prudent, as they say: threatening cliffs, beyond imagination; impossible even to consider returning. I traded everything I had for food; my shoes, my wrist watch, my key chain with all my keys (I wouldn't be needing them now), a fountain pen that was almost out of ink.

The only thing of any value I have left is my polaroid camera; no one wanted it. Up here they don't believe in preserving images; just the opposite: every day they strive to create new images, they invent new images only for the moment. Often they get together to tell one another about the incorporeal images they've been entertaining. They sit in a circle on the dirt floor in the darkness of their communal building – a kind of hut – and concentrate on making the vision appear. One day, out of nothing, they materialized a tapestry of non-existent colors and ineffable design, but they decided that it was but a pale reflection of the mental image, and they broke the circle in order to return the tapestry to the nothingness from which it had come.

They are strange creatures; normally they speak a language whose meaning they themselves have forgotten. They communicate by interpreting pauses, intonations, facial expressions, and sighs. I tried to learn this language of silences, but it seems that my tongue is not meant for such subtleties. At any rate, they speak our language when they refer to trivial matters, the daily needs that have nothing to do with their images. Even so, some words are missing from their vocabulary. For example, they have no word for yesterday or tomorrow, before and after, or one of these days. Here everything is now, and always. An unsatisfactory imitation of eternity, like the tapestry I've already mentioned. Have mentioned? Oh, yes, I'm the only one that uses that verb tense; I may also be the only one who has any notion of conjugations. A vice left over from the world down there, knowledge I can't trade anyone, because no one wants it. ◆

Untouched by modernity: a farm in the Andean highlands of Ecuador.

Photo: P. Frey

from UP AMONG THE EAGLES
by Luisa Valenzuela, Argentina

– Kishwar Naheed has a message
for 'masters of countries with
a cold climate' –

MY COUNTRY IS TORRID
maybe that is why my hands feel warm
My country is torrid
maybe that is why my feet burn
My country is torrid
maybe that is why there are boils on my body
My country is torrid
maybe that is why the roof of my house
    melted and caved in.

My country is torrid
maybe that is why my children are kept thirsty
My country is torrid
maybe that is why I am kept unclothed.

My country is torrid
maybe that is why one neither knows of clouds
    which bring rainfall
nor of floods that destroy.
And to wreck my harvests, sometimes moneylenders,
sometimes wild beasts, sometimes calamities
and sometimes self-styled masters arrive.

Don't teach me to hate my torrid country
Let me dry my wet clothes in these courtyards
let me plant gold in its fields
let me quench my thirst at its rivers
let me rest beneath the shade of its trees
let me wear its dust and wrap its distances around me.
I don't want the shade of lengthening shadows
I have the support of the rays of the rising sun.
The sun has made its energy accessible for my country
the sun and I
the sun and you
cannot walk side by side
The sun has chosen *me* for company.

TO MASTERS OF COUNTRIES WITH A COLD CLIMATE
by Kishwar Naheed, Pakistan

environment

Pathan woman bearing a load of firewood for cooking. Photos of women in the North-West Frontier province of Pakistan are few and far between. The fact that a woman was holding the camera probably helped.

Photo: S. Errington/ Hutchison

*– Anees Jung
on the allegiances
of city-dwellers –*

d ESPITE THE EMERGING LURE of the cities, return to the village is a recurring theme in the life of every city dweller. Whether a woman vendor plying her trade on a street or a taxi driver or a business man who has earned his thousands, the village remains a vital and organic link with his or her social reality. Even the most urbane Indian refers to his village as 'back home'. Marriage alliances continue to be arranged with certain castes and religious groups that have roots in the village. Whether it is to announce the birth of a son or his coming of age, to introduce a bride to the community or to observe ceremonies connected with a death in the family, people try and return to the village. In some ways, this return not only balances but assimilates the disruption and dissonance created by the city. Even in a metropolis like Bombay, where half of the city's population lives in slums, defined as rich, poor, permanent and shifting, migrants jealously preserve identities of faith, language, culture. In Dharavi, a slum that has the dubious reputation of being the largest in South-east Asia, survives a potters' colony that sets aside a day for worship of the wheel. In the slums of Dadar, migrants from Tamil Nadu celebrate their native Pongal, while those from Gujarat light up the smog-filled sky with kites on the day of Sankaranti. On the day of Janmashtami, young men, scattered in the city, find each other to dance the way they did back in the villages. ◆

Have chicken will travel. The ability to pick up roots – and assets – and migrate is for many Indians the key to survival.

Photo: B. Bosshart

from **UNVEILING INDIA**
by Anees Jung, India

*– Aman on how she came
into this world,
as a nomad –*

MY MAMA AND GRANDMAMA had been travelling for a couple of days, walking miles and miles with their animals, searching for water. Mama was nine months pregnant. When you live out in the bush with animals – goats, sheep, camels, cows – you've got to find water and grass for them. So people go where water is or where rain has fallen – you have to follow the rain. We call that *sahan*: the look for water. It can take days and days, sometimes, just to find where there is water.

Mama and Grandmama stopped for the night, and made breakfast in the morning. They were on the move again, when her labour pains started. I was on my way. It was late in the day – the time when the heat of noon is gone and the land looks beautiful in the long, low rays of the afternoon sun. My Mama knew her labour had begun, but didn't want to stop because there were a lot of people travelling together. My Grandmama had already seen her holding her stomach, and my mama had told her that labour had started. As the sun went down, her labour pains began to be closer together, but still she didn't want to stop. Finally, after the sun went down, they reached the place where they had planned to set up camp for the night. Mama told Grandmama to set up the house quickly, because it was time, she was about to have the baby, and besides, it was nearly dark. So they put up the bush house fast – in about half an hour, because women in the same group help each other. They made a big fire outside the door of the house so that the light would shine inside and they could see while the baby was being born. Grandmama had helped Mama give birth to all her children, and there were two other women to help. When the baby was ready to be born, the two women held Mama under her arms, in a standing position, and Grandmama sat between Mama's legs with a knife to do the cut with and to catch the baby when it came out. About half an hour after they got everything ready, I was born.

In the morning they were on the move again, with Mama bleeding. She had a little girl! That's how she had me – while they were on the move. It was beautiful.

The next day, they reached the place where the water was. The women and the children were tired. They saw a nice big thorn tree, and they stopped beside it. They let the camels sit and drink, to relax a little bit. And then it began to rain. When it rains in the desert, everything smells good. When you look around – everywhere – the plants begin to grow. A lot of different flowers were there, flowers that nobody planted – Allah planted – white ones, red ones, purple ones – wildflowers all around them. Everything turned green and life was back to normal.

When he heard about me, my daddy sent word to mama that she wasn't divorced – because she had a baby now. Men talk nicely when there is a baby involved. My Mama and my daddy were still married after all, and that's how, after a year, my sister Sharifa was born.

My mother still refused to accept what my father wanted, which was for him to be the boss. He wanted to put her animals together with his animals – everything together. My mother didn't want that, and that was the reason they finally did divorce. My daddy was in love with her, but he had his pride. Everyone respected him and he didn't see why she couldn't respect him too, after having two of his children...

When I first remember things, I remember being out in the bush. We were not staying in one place, we were moving, moving, moving. I would wake up and see Mama taking our home apart, and the camel sitting there for her to put the house on. Everybody was doing the same thing. Because we're a group, we move as a group, not as a family – maybe eight families, ten families, fifteen families... we all move together. When we were ready to move, the women would break their homes up. They tied the camels together by their tails, and they all walked in a line, with one person leading in the front. All the camels have a rope around their necks and the first person in the line just holds the rope and pulls, and the camels *galug, galug...* they have a bell around the neck, and we walk along, with just that sound: *galug, galug, galug, galug.*

You have to keep moving your animals in the country, because cows eat a lot of grass and camels eat the leaves off the trees →

The nomadic way of life is under greater threat today than ever before, as governments try to 'settle' nomads. This woman is a Baluchi and her community moves through eastern Iran, Afghanistan and Pakistan with their herds of sheep. The women are gifted carpet weavers.

Photo: N. Kasraian

After they eat everything, you have to move them to the next place where the grass is not touched yet. We move along, and even the camels seem small, because the flat land seems to stretch out forever — as far as your eye can see it reaches out to where the sky begins. We walk along over the dusty, dry, sandy land until we find somewhere nice and green. When you're moving from place to place, everything you have has to go on one camel. So those houses in the country have to be easy to move. When you get to where you plan to stay, you dig a hole, making a design with your feet, making a circle as big as you want your home. You have a frame made of long branches bound together and curved, like a beehive, and you cover that with woven mats made of straw or grass. You hang an old cloth at the front and that's your door. You can get in and out and it's nice and cool. You put a mat or sheet inside, and you sleep. Since you don't have a suitcase, you keep your belongings and clothes wrapped up in a bag, and you use that as a pillow. Or you might even grab a sack of beans or corn anything you want just to hold you. It's a simple life.

And in the morning you hear *chickee, chickee, chickee, moo* and *aaa*, and it's beautiful. Everything comes alive. Everything gets up one at a time. Early in the morning they milk the cows, the goats. Then it's breakfast time. We have milk with hot grits or popped corn with milk — they burn the corn in the fire *bum bup, buppa*: popped corn. If we have sugar, we make tea. The older boys take the cows and goats away to find something to eat. The young children go with their mamas, or with the girls who are going to watch the small baby goats or the small baby cows. In the evening everyone comes back together and we cook a big meal. We eat meat that the women have dried and we put beans and white corn together and make a dish we call *amboolo*.

After the meal, if they want, the big boys and girls dance. I was about four or five when we were in the country, but I remember I went with the big boys and girls. We'd collect a lot of wood in the evening so we could have a big fire. Most of the time we'd sing and talk. With the fire and the smoke, the flies and mosquitoes go away. We sit around the fire. We're just wild kids, in this beautiful place. We dance and we have fun. That is my first memory. ◆

from **AMAN. THE STORY OF A SOMALI GIRL**
by Aman, Somalia

 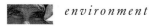

IT STARTS EARLY — sexual discrimination. As the girl in Mrinal Pande's story finds out doing battle with her male cousins. The various strands of prejudice and inequality often weave themselves into a complex mesh for women. There are divisions of class and the hypocrisies that breed therein, exposed by Isabel Allende. Or there's *politics and* the issue of race, explored in a no-nonsense poem from South *society* Africa. Andrée Chedid meanwhile, uses humour to relate a moment when religion and a woman's rights clash most noisily. And, of course, there's colonialism — for women have been colonized in so many ways. But meek acceptance is absent here. Women are speaking out clearly in their own, determined voices!

*i*T IS MY CELEBRATION
I will drum my drum
I will sing my song
I will dance my dance
I do not need your anaemic hands
brought together in pale applause
I do not need your
'You are such musical people'
toothy smile
It is my celebration
You wonder what I have to celebrate
What does the drum tell me
If you must speculate
Watch out
One day as you throw your head back
As you gather your hearty laughter
I will change my dance
I will still sing
The drum will scream
Celebration.

*Independence
celebrations at
Windhoek, Namibia.
The country was the
last colony in Africa
to gain freedom.*

*Photo: J. Matthews/
Network*

I WILL STILL SING

by Amelia Blossom Pegram, South Africa

– Ester, a 'mother of the disappeared' in Guatemala, talks to Margaret Hooks –

I HAVE JUST BEEN LOOKING through some of my son's papers, his study records, personal things... I like to do this when I have some free time, to remind me of him. Not that I don't remember him, but this helps me to keep his image alive in my mind. I only do it when I feel really strong and know that it won't make me cry.

My son, Jorge Alberto Herrate, was abducted on 15 May 1983. It was during the regime of General Efraín Ríos Montt, of which we have terrible memories. He was dragged out of this house in front of my husband and me. It was about 6.40 pm but it was still light outside. It had been a very hot day so we had the front door open. I was still in the kitchen and we had just finished supper. My son was watching television when the men came into the house without saying a word. There were two of them. My son is not very tall, about 5ft 5in. These men were tall and armed. As they were the ones with the guns and our door was open it was pointless to try and hide. One trained his enormous gun on us from the doorway. Although they were wearing civilian clothes, which is common in these cases, they belonged to the government security forces. The only words spoken were when the man who was pointing his gun at us told us to close the door. I ran after him into the garden to see what was happening. I tried to grab hold of my son, but I was threatened by the other man with his gun. They took him away in a small mustard-coloured car. I saw three other cars behind the house, one of which was a large, elegant dark-coloured one, and I also saw more armed men... The neighbours and passers-by witnessed everything because it was still daylight. But it is difficult to ask people to testify because it is very risky.

My son was working for the Western Oil petroleum company at the time. He had just come home the day before. He worked out on the site (at Rubelsalto in the Peten) for three weeks at a time, then he would get a week off... He was 29 years old and married.

His wife and two little girls weren't here that night. They were in Chicago visiting his wife's family and were due back the following day. They came as planned and stayed until November. But Magda, my daughter-in-law, couldn't find a job that paid enough here, so what with that and the personal insecurity she went to the United States. In Guatemala she ran the risk of being abducted as well and of something awful happening to her children.

As soon as they had taken my son, my husband went straight to the police to report it. He went to all the different police forces and, as they usually do in these cases, they all said they would investigate. The next day we went to see a lawyer to draw up a declaration to take to the Tribunal Tower. The judge who attended to us made us pay 50 *quetzales*, which is completely illegal, but you think that by paying the money you will get some sort of response...

On 19 May my children who live in the United States went to Americas Watch, to the Washington Office on Latin America, and to US congressmen to denounce what had happened. I went to the Venezuelan and Canadian embassies here. I knew that the petroleum companies belong to these countries, so I went to beg them to do something, to intercede with the Guatemalan government so that my son might reappear. I also had meetings with Lord Colville [then UN Special Rapporteur on Guatemala] when he visited here to ask him to intervene and help find my son. It was all totally useless...

I went to the morgues; I saw hundreds of corpses... I spent ten months going around the morgues. I had mixed feelings about it: I wanted to find something, even if it was only his body, but at the same time I prayed that he was still alive. When I saw the atrocities and the mutilated bodies, it sent shivers down my spine. I felt so depressed that I thought I would lose my mind... ◆

from **UNTIL WE FIND THEM**
Ester, from Guatemala, was intervieved by Margaret Hooks

'Why so much hate... that they vent their spleen on tormenting a child!' – placard held by a mother in Guatemala City. The country is emerging from years of violence. Thousands 'disappeared' – abducted by the army, tortured and killed.

Photo: V. Olmi

– Isabel Allende's Clara
is taken out for a bit
of political education –

*a*T TIMES CLARA would accompany her mother and two or three of her suffragette friends on their visits to factories, where they would stand on soapboxes and make speeches to the women who worked there while the foremen and bosses, snickering and hostile, observed them from a prudent distance. Despite her tender age and complete ignorance of matters of this world, Clara grasped the absurdity of the situation and wrote in her notebook about the contrast of her mother and her friends, in their fur coats and suede boots, speaking of oppression, equality, and rights to a sad, resigned group of hard-working women in denim aprons, their hands red with chilblains. From the factory the ladies would move on to the tearoom on the Plaza de Armas, where they would stop for tea and pastry and discuss the progress of their campaign, not for a moment letting this frivolous distraction divert them from their flaming ideals. At other times her mother would take her to the slums on the outskirts of the city or to the tenements, where they arrived with their car piled high with food and with clothes that [her mother] Nívea and her friends sewed for the poor. On these occasions too, the child wrote with formidable intuition that charity had no effect on such monumental injustice. ◆

from **THE HOUSE OF THE SPIRITS**
by Isabel Allende, Chile

The gap between rich and poor remains vast in Latin America, and prospects for working class or peasant girls are generally limited to working as servants in the houses of middle- and upper-class city dwellers. These girls are from Ecuador.

Photo: W. Germann

– Mrinal Pande explores
the trials of being
'a daughter's daughter' –

aFTERNOON IS STORYTIME, siesta time. The Enemies have reached Grandmother's four-poster before we do. A whispered whine, a subtle flick of head towards our approach. Grandmother's room smells of camphor and cats and Huxley's Wintogino balm. Anu lies next to her, fiddling with her locket which has a photograph of our dead grandfather inside.

'You sit there. You are Daughter's children! We'll sleep here near Grandmother.' Anu points at the foot of the bed with his foot. Shubha nods vigorously in assent.

The wise General retreats when needs be. Dinu and I sit as directed.

'What is this about a peacock?' Grandmother asks between a yawn and a click of the betelnut in her mouth. She looks at both of us with a smile that says, Give-It-To-Them-They-Are-Your-Cousins-After-All-And-It-Is-Their-House...

'It's ours.'

'No, it's our home, it's ours.'

'Why don't you give it to them — only for a while,' says Grandmother. Her tone says we are not to complain but give it. Now. We will have to do the best we can. But still...

'Won't! He will never return it.' Dinu holds her ground with an obstinacy I could hug her for. Her eyes are bright with unshed tears. I feel weepy for her but I know better than to speak or to call Grandmother's or anyone's attention to me. Younger sisters can always get teased for being younger sisters. For me to stand up openly for Dinu just now would not only be disloyal but also troublesome. I understand Warfare, I do my best. Although we were forever being told not to do things alone and being given the example of seven brothers who even distributed a sesame seed equally among themselves, we know better than to surrender our treasure in this house to the son's children. We'll never get it back. Grandmother gives us a long reproachful look. Anu whimpers. Shubha whines.

I'm beginning to find this War tiring — the weight of sins of holding back, or hiding, of not wishing to share, brings tears to my eyes. Can't we ever hold on to our things? We, whose father has no parents, no house, and is forever getting transferred, we know a lot about losing things. Every few months we move around with our trunks and holdalls, from city to city, suburb to suburb. Even if Anu and his sister come here only during summer, have they not always had this house waiting for them to hoard all their goodies within? Exotic presents that people bring them: marbles, dolls, kites, clips, ribbons. They are all kept for them in locked *almirahs* by doting aunts. They have several toffee tins and drawers full of stones, feathers, acorns, chestnuts and coloured tinfoil. We lose ours with each transfer. And now they want the Magic Peacock!

It just was not fair.

'Don't worry, my ruby!' Grandmother tells Anu. 'We will get you another one. A better one.'

She glances at us. Her eyes saying, Give! Give! Give!

We both smile back sweetly. Our eyes say, No! No! No!

Grandmother's eyes cloud over and icily she begins,

'Once upon a time...' ◆

from **DAUGHTER'S DAUGHTER**
by Mrinal Pande, India

The look of defiance. Girls are still viewed very much as 'second best' in much of India. But the women's movement is strong on grassroots action against child marriages, dowry deaths and other injustices.

Photo: B. Bosshart

tHE LONG LINE OF BLOOD
and family ties

An African countenance here
A European countenance there
An Amerindian cast of cheek
An Asianic turn of eye
And the tongue's salty accommodation
The tapestry is mine
All the bloodstained prints
The scatterlinks
The grafting strand of crinkled hair
The black persistent blooming

TAPESTRY

by Grace Nichols, Guyana

*Cubans
relaxing in their
Havana home.
Caribbean islanders
can lay claim to a
mixture of different
ancestries – African,
Amerindian and
European.*

*Photo: T. Hopker/
Magnum*

*a*ND WHEN THEY WOULD ASK
what are you going to be when you grow up
and without thinking, I would answer
wait on people in a store just like this one
and they would laugh at such a meager dream
they hadn't travelled so much
so the granddaughter would end up, like them
behind the counter.
And they would send me off to study,
because one who studies
even if she's a woman, succeeds.

*A café on Peru's
desert coast road, the
Pacific Highway.
Small food shops
and restaurants serve
the needs of bus
travellers as well as
the inhabitants of
coastal oases.*

Photo: M. Paoluzzo

THE GROCER'S DREAM
by Giovanna Pollarolo, Peru

WE ARE ALL MOTHERS,
and we have that fire within us,
of powerful women
whose spirits are so angry
we can laugh beauty into life
and still make you taste
the salty tears of our knowledge –
For we are not tortured
anymore;
we have seen beyond your lies and disguises,
and we have mastered the language of words,
we have mastered speech.
And know
we have also seen ourselves raw
and naked piece by piece until our flesh lies flayed
with blood on our own hands.
What terrible thing can you do to us
which we have not done to ourselves?
What can you tell us
which we didn't deceive ourselves with
a long time ago?
You cannot know how long we cried
until we laughed
over the broken pieces of our dreams.

Ignorance
shattered us into such fragments
we had to unearth ourselves piece by piece,
to recover with our own hands such unexpected relics
even we wondered
how we would hold such treasure.
Yes, we have conceived
to forge our mutilated hopes
into the substance of visions
beyond your imaginings
to declare the pain of our deliverance:
So do not even ask,
do not ask what it is we are labouring with *this* time;
Dreamers remember their dreams
when they are disturbed –
And you shall not escape
what we *will* make
of the broken pieces of our lives.

LIBERATION
by Abena Busia, Ghana

102 *politics and society*

This woman comes from Eastern Ghana. The country gained its independence from British rule in 1957. But democratic freedom did not follow and the country has been plagued by the political power of its own military. The struggle to achieve genuine democracy continues.

Photo: R. Schmid

– Suniti Namjoshi
on womanliness –

IN THEIR EXTREME OLD AGE a childless couple was granted a daughter. This made them very happy, and they prayed to the gods every morning and evening to bless their child. The prayer was granted. As their daughter grew up it soon became obvious that she was a remarkable child. She could run further and faster than anyone in the village, her manners were good, she sang rather well, and she excelled in her studies. There was only one thing wrong, which spoilt everything. This was not a defect. The gods hadn't cheated. She was indeed blessed with great ability. But everyone in the village was critical of her.

'To be so damned good,' they said, 'is not womanly.' ◆

Keeping the spark alive. Perhaps this Indian girl will be able to carry her natural spontaneous energy into womanhood?

Photo: Ed Brouns

THE GODS
by Suniti Namjoshi, India

– *Andrée Chedid's fertile woman does battle with the local holy man* –

*t*HE DOOR CLOSED, Amina turned toward her stove of pressed earth. No amount of fatigue could bend her back. She had that sovereign carriage of Egyptian peasants which makes the head seem always to balance and carry a fragile and heavy burden.

Was she young? Hardly thirty! But what good is youth, if no care is taken for it?

At the stove, the woman leaned forward to draw from a nook the bread for the week, rolled in jute cloth. A few dried olives lying in a bowl, two strings of onions hanging on the wall. The woman counted the flatcakes, hefted them; she placed them against her cheek to test their freshness. Having chosen the two best, she dusted them with the back of her sleeve, blew upon them. Then, taking them as an offering, between her open hands, she advanced again to the door.

The presence of the [holy man] delighted her. Her hut seemed less wretched, her children less squalling, and the voice of [her husband] Zekr more lively, more animated.

On the way she bumped into two of her children. One hung upon her skirts, stretching up to seize a flatcake:

'Give me. I'm hungry.'

'Go away, Barsoum. It's not for you. Let go!'

'I'm not Barsoum. I'm Ahmed.' The darkness of the room obscured their faces.

'I'm hungry!'

She shoved him back. The child slipped, fell, rolled upon the earth and howled.

Feeling herself at fault, she hastened forward, pushed the door open quickly, crossed the threshold. She closed the door immediately and leaned back against it with all her weight. Her face sweaty, her mouth pressed shut, she stood motionless, facing the old man and her husband, and drew breath deeply into her lungs.

'The eucalyptus under which I repose, which grows in the midst of a field of oats...' began Hadj Osman.

'It is still there,' sighed the woman.

'The last time, it seemed very sickly.'

'It's still there,' she replied. 'Here, nothing ever changes. Nothing at all.'

What she had just said gave her a sudden wish to cry and to complain. The old man could hear her; he might console her, perhaps? But for what? She didn't know exactly. 'For everything,' she thought to herself.

'Take these cakes. They are for you!'

The empty water jug lay upon the ground. Hadj Osman took the flatcakes from the hands of the woman and thanked her. He slipped one of the cakes between his robe and the skin of his chest; he bit into the other. He chewed diligently, making each mouthful last a long time.

Pleased to see him regain strength because of her bread, Amina smiled once again. Then, remembering that her husband objected severely to her remaining any length of time outside the house, she took leave of the two men, bowing to them.

'May Allah heap blessings upon you!' the old man exclaimed. 'May he bless you and grant you seven more children!'

The woman pressed against the wall to keep from staggering, she shrank into her large, black clothing, she hid her face.

'What's the matter? Are you ill?' the old man asked.

She was unable to form the words. At last she blurted out:

'I have nine children already, holy man, I beg you withdraw your benediction.'

He thought he must have misunderstood; she articulated so poorly:

'What did you say? Repeat.'

'Take back your benediction, I beg you.'

'I don't understand you,' interrupted the old man. 'You don't know what you are saying.'

Her face still buried in her hands, the woman shook her head from right to left, from left to right:

'No, No!.. Enough!.. It is enough!'

All around children metamorphosed into grasshoppers, bounded against her, encircled her, transformed her into a clod of earth, inert. Their hundreds of hands became claws, nettles twitched →

Bedouin women come together to spin – and chat – in rural Egypt.

Photo: S. Errington/ Hutchison

her clothes, tearing her flesh.

'No, no!... I can't endure any more!'

She choked:

'Take back the benediction!'

Zekr, petrified by her aplomb, stood facing her, not opening his mouth.

'The benedictions come from the hand of God, I can change nothing in them.'

'You can... you *must* take them back!'

With a smirk of disdain, Hadj Osman turned his head away.

But she continued to harass him:

'Take back the benediction! Speak to me. You must take back the benediction.'

She clenched her fists and advanced towards him:

'You must reply to me!'

The old man pushed her back with both hands:

'Nothing. I withdraw nothing.'

She reared, advanced again. Was she the same woman of but a few moments ago?

'Take back the benediction,' she hurled.

From what source had she got that look, that voice?

'What use is it to tame the waters? What good are the promised harvests? Here, everywhere there will be thousands of other mouths to feed! Have you looked at our children? What do they look like to you! If you only looked at them!'

Opening wide the door of her hovel, she called in:

'Barsoum, Fatma, Osman, Naghi! Come. Come, all of you. The bigger ones carry the smaller ones in their arms. Come out, all nine. Show yourselves!'

'You are mad!'

'Show your arms, your shoulders! Lift your dress, show your stomachs, your thighs, your knees!'

'You deny life!' the old man sneered.

'Don't talk to me about life! You know nothing about life!'

'Children – they are life!'

'Too many children – they are death!'

'Amina, you blaspheme!'

'I call upon God!'

'God will not hear you.'

'He will hear me!'

'If I were your husband, I'd chastize you.'

'No one, today, no one will lift a hand to me. No one!' She seized the moving arm of Hadj Osman:

'Not even you!... Take back the benediction or I will not let loose.'

She shook him to force him to recall his words:

'Do what I tell you: take back the benediction!'

'You are possessed! Get back; don't touch me again. I withdraw nothing!'

Even though the old man had several times called upon him to speak, Zekr remained mute and immobile. Then, brusquely, he moved.

Would he hurl himself upon Amina and beat her, as he usually did?

'You Zekr, on your knees! Now you! You make him understand. Beg him! With me.'

The words had come from her! How had she dared to say them? and with such an imperious tone? Suddenly, seized with a trembling, strangled with old fears, she unclenched her fists; her limbs grew soft as cotton. Elbows raised to protect herself from blows, she shrivelled against the wall.

'The woman is right, holy man. Take back the benediction.'

She couldn't believe her ears. Nor her eyes. Zekr had heard her. Zekr was there on his knees at the feet of the old man.

Alerted by the clamour, neighbours came running in from all sides. Zekr sought the eye of Amina kneeling beside him; the woman was overwhelmed with gratitude.

'Holy man, take back the benediction,' the two implored together. A tight circle formed about them. Feeling himself supported by that crowd, the old man stretched up on his toes and raised a menacing index finger:

'This man, this woman reject the work of God. They sin! Drive them out. Else an evil will fall upon the village!' →

'Seven children! He has ordained seven more children upon us! What can we do?' groaned Amina.

Fatma, her cousin, already had eight. Soad, six. Fathia, who always accompanied her younger sister of the rotten teeth and the wild eyes, had four sons and three daughters. And the others? It was the same story... Yet, each of the women, fearful, hesitant, looked mistrustfully at Amina.

'Births are in God's hands,' said Fatma, seeking the approbation of the old man – and of the other men.

'It's up to us to decide whether we want children,' proclaimed Zekr, leaping up.

'That's blasphemy,' protested Khalifé, a young man with protruding ears. 'Something bad will happen to us!'

'Drive them out!' the old man insisted. 'They profane the place.'

Amina put her hand fraternally upon her husband's shoulder.

'We must listen to Hadj Osman; he's a holy man,' murmured a few disturbed voices.

'No, it is I you must listen to!' cried Zekr. 'I who am like all of you. It's Amina you must listen to, Amina who is a woman like other women. How could she bear seven more children? What could we do?'

His cheeks were aflame. From way back someone made a timid echo: 'What will they do?'

From mouth to mouth those words swelled: 'What will they do?'

'No more children!' suddenly uttered a blind little girl clinging to her mother's skirts.

What was happening to this village, to these people, to this valley? Hadj Osman sadly shook his head.

'No more children!' the voices repeated.

Swinging between his crutches, Mahmoud the one-legged approached the old man and whispered to him:

'Take back your benediction.'

'I withdraw nothing!'

Pushing with his elbows to disengage himself from the crowd, the holy man spat out curses; and with an angry motion he upset the cripple, who lost hold of his crutches and rolled to the ground.

That was the signal.

Fikhry threw himself upon the old man. To avenge the one-legged man, Zekr struck also. Salah, whipping the air with his bamboo cane approached. It was a sarabande of motion and cries. Hoda ran in with a piece of garden hose. A little boy pulled up a boundary stake. An elderly man broke a branch from a weeping willow and entered into the melee.

'No more children!'

'Take back your benediction!'

'We won't endure any more!'

'We want to live.'

'Live!'

Towards evening the police found Hadj Osman stretched out, face down, next to a trampled flatcake and a water jug broken into bits. They raised him up, brushed off his garments, and took him to the nearest dispensary.

The next day, a police raid took place in the village. The men who had taken part in the melee were driven off in a paddy wagon. The vehicle bounced off, down the long tow-path which led to the police station.

Eyes shining, Amina and her companions gathered at the edge of the village, stared a long while down the road. Clouds of dust rose and spread.

Their husbands weren't really going away, leaving them behind... never had they felt themselves so close together. Never.

That day was not a day like all other days.

That day, the long trial had reached its end. ◆

from THE LONG TRIAL
by Andrée Chedid, Egypt

– Kebbedesh, a guerrilla, talks about what made her a fighter –

MY FAMILY WERE PEASANTS. I never knew my father – he was murdered by outlaws when my mother was pregnant with me. My mother faced many problems after his death. She was shocked and her health was not good. Because of her troubles she called me Kebbedesh, 'a heavy burden'.

After a while my mother remarried. She left for another village but I went to live with my aunts. When I was seven, my aunts arranged for me to be married to a wealthy neighbour. He was rich, chauvinistic and rather foolish. He was huge, with a beard, and he seemed like a giant to me. My uncles told him not to have sex with me. They made him promise in front of a priest that he would wait until I was mature, but this did not work.

I went to his house, which was strange to me. I saw him for the first time inside the house. He was like a giant, like something that makes you afraid. At that time I didn't know what marriage, or being husband and wife, meant. After three terrible nights I escaped back to my aunt's house. My family insulted me, shouted at me, 'Why did you come back, you stupid girl?' They forced me to return.

After some weeks I escaped again, this time to the forest. I passed several very difficult days there. I was hungry and thirsty and I just wanted to die. I fainted and a peasant found me and took me back to his house. He knew me and knew my family were angry so he kept me in his house. He gave me milk because I couldn't eat *injera* [fermented grain pancake, the basic food of the region]. After a few days he took me back to my home. My family took me in but then they tried to persuade me to return to my husband. They said he was rich and owned many cattle. They wanted me to go and live with him again.

They took me to him for the third time. I lived there for some months, maybe a year, but then I escaped again. I felt it was too difficult to live in the world. I took a rope and went to the forest to hang myself. A neighbouring peasant who was tending his cattle in the forest found me standing under a tree. He was surprised and asked me what I was doing there with a rope. I told him I was collecting wood. He didn't believe me and tried to take me back to my husband. I refused to go – I said I was looking for wood.

After two days in the forest, I became so hungry that I returned to a neighbour's house. They tried to reconcile me to my family. When I was eight, one year after I was married, they made me return to my so-called husband. My husband forced me to have sex when I was eight years old. I was sick for many days after that. I just didn't know what to do or how to help myself. All paths seemed closed to me. All the people in the area were against me. They said I should stay with my husband because he was rich. They couldn't see it from my point of view – they thought it was natural.

I continued like this until I was eleven, escaping and being returned by my family. At last my mother learned what was happening to me. She came back to the village, divorced me from that man and took me away with her to her village.

But once I was there I faced another problem. The people there insulted me. Because I didn't know my father, they said I was undisciplined. They said I was rubbish because I had been brought up by a woman, without a father. They said a woman could not bring up a child properly, that I was undisciplined to divorce my husband and so they teased and insulted me. Things weren't easy for my mother either. She also felt insulted because I had left my husband. So I decided to go to Asmara. A friend had come to visit us from Asmara, so I went to her and begged her to take me away with her. I was fifteen at that time.

But when I reached Asmara I didn't like it. There was nothing for me there. After a miserable time there I went to T'senay near the Sudan border and got a job in a bar. In the bar I was badly treated – men came and kicked me, spat in my face. They could do whatever they wanted. The owner of the bar also was cruel. If I broke a glass she would not pay me. I worked there for two years but was not even able to buy any clothes. The male customers cheated me. They said they would give me money to pass the night with me, but after they slept they would leave without paying.

At last some women came to the bar from Sudan. They had →

jewellery and good clothes so I asked them about their life in the Sudan. They encouraged me to go there with them, saying I could have a good life. So I went to Sudan after two years in T'senay. I lived in the Sudan for ten years. I rented a room and worked as a prostitute for ten miserable years. The life of prostitution is clear to you, so I don't need to explain it.

In 1977, TPLF members were trying to agitate the people in Sudan and to establish underground movements wherever there were Tigrayans. I became interested in this news. TPLF didn't need to politicize me – I had led a terrible life. No one knew more about women's oppression than I did. I became an active participant in TPLF activities and worked for two years with them. I learned sewing and then, in 1980, I decided to come to the Field as a fighter. After I finished training, I was assigned to the workshop as a tailor. Then, three years ago, I was assigned here to Marta School. I am a student and I teach sewing. I am also a fighter.

I feel proud and happy to be here. We are many women with different miserable experiences. We discuss our past lives all the time. This gives me a very special feeling. Before I came here I was fighting without a full consciousness. I understood more than anyone that women are oppressed by men and by class oppression, but still I was not fighting consciously. I had not examined the 'woman question' scientifically. Since coming here I have studied the 'woman question' and have come to realize that the solution is to struggle and to bring about a new society.

It makes me happy that I came both to learn and to teach. I feel so happy to be teaching my sisters, to be producing skilled sisters. I feel joy and happiness when I see the results of my teaching. ◆

from SWEETER THAN HONEY:
TESTIMONIES OF TIGRAYAN WOMEN
by Kebbedesh, Tigray

politics and society

endpiece

*– Violeta Parra's gutsy
hymn to life –*

I THANK LIFE FOR SO MANY GIFTS,
for my mind's windows, which I open
to see clearly, black and white,
the starred depths of the sky
and the man I love, lost in the crowd.

I thank life for so many gifts,
for my hearing that night and day
and all around records crickets,
canaries, hammers, turbines, barking,
squalls and my sweetheart's tender voice.

I thank life for so many gifts,
for sounds, the alphabet, and
the words I think and speak –
mother, friend, brother, and light
shining on the path of my lover's soul.

I thank life for so many gifts,
for the tread of my tired feet
wandering through cities and puddles,
beaches and deserts, mountains and plains,
your house, your street, and your garden.

I thank life for so many gifts,
for my heart which shakes its frame
as I see the fruits of the human brain,
and I face good so far from evil,
and I look into your deep clear eyes.

I thank life for so many gifts,
for laughter and tears, telling me
what is luck and what misfortune,
the two elements of my song
and your song – the same song,
and everyone's song – my own.

I thank life for so many gifts.

I THANK LIFE FOR SO MANY GIFTS
by Violeta Parra of Chile

114   *endpiece*

*The nature-loving,
indigenous people of
South America were
close to the heart of
Chilean poet and
singer Violeta Parra.
This Quechua
Indian woman lives
in what is now Peru
but is descended
from the Incas who
inhabited the length
of the Andes from
Colombia in the
north to Chile
in the South.*

*Photo: S. Errington/
Hutchison*

Assumpta Acam-Oturu
UGANDA

was born in 1953 in Teso, Eastern Uganda. She obtained a Diploma in Journalism from Mindolo Ecumenical Centre's School of Journalism in Zambia and a BA in Journalism and International Relations from the University of Southern California. She now works for a radio station in Los Angeles. Her poems have appeared in *Ufahamu*.

Omega Agüero
CUBA

was born in 1940 in Camaguey, Cuba. She has worked as an actress and a teacher. Her first book *La Alegre vida campestre* (The Good Life in the Country) won the David Prize for short stories in 1973. *A Man, A Woman* is taken from her collection of short stories *El Muro de medio metro* published in 1977. Her works have been included in anthologies in East Germany, Bulgaria, Czechoslovakia and the Ukraine. Omega Agüero's stories deal with a range of situations, the early work focusing largely on peasant life and the problems of women in Cuba before the Revolution. In her latest work she explores themes of remembrance and the world of dreams.

Ama Ata Aidoo
GHANA

was born in 1942 near Dominase in Central Ghana. She had a distinguished academic career, lecturing at the University of Cape Coast, before being appointed Ghanaian Minister of Education until 1983. She has written a number of novels, poetry and plays, including *Changes, Our Sister Killjoy, No Sweetness Here* and the play *The Dilemma of a Ghost*. Since 1983 she has lived and worked mainly abroad and is currently in exile in Zimbabwe with her daughter Kinna. She was Chair of the Africa Regional Panel for the Common-wealth Writers' Prize in 1989-90.

Malak'Abd al-Aziz
EGYPT

was born in 1935. At seventeen she published her first book, *Aghani al-Siba* (Songs of Youth). A prolific critic, poet and writer, her subsequent books include: *Qala al-Masa'* (The Night Narrated); *Bahr al-Samt* (Sea of Silence); *Ann Almisa Qalb al-Ahya'* (That I Touch the Heart of Things); and *Ughniyat li-l-Layl* (Songs of the Night). Some of her poems have been included in *The Longman Anthology of World Literature by Women: 1875-1975*.

Isabel Allende
CHILE

was born in Lima, Peru in 1942 but con-siders Chile her native country. She lived there from childhood until her uncle, the socialist President Salvador Allende, was overthrown in a bloody military coup in 1973. She fled the country and went into exile in Venezuela. For several years she pursued the career in journalism she had started at the age of 17. Then in 1981 she turned her hand to writing a novel. The result was *The House of the Spirits*, which became an instant, worldwide best-seller. This novel alone has made her the most widely-read Latin American woman writer of all time. It was followed by *Of Love and Shadows, Eva Luna*, and *The Stories of Eva Luna*. Her latest book, *Paula*, is the true account of her own daughter who went into a coma several years ago. Isabel Allende now lives in California.

Aman

SOMALIA

was born into a nomadic family in the 1950s. Her story, told to Canadian anthropologist Janice Boddy, is an intimate first-person account of a young woman's coming of age in the harsh, deeply traditional, war-torn country. Her life has been dramatic in the extreme, from her birth in the bush, to her forced and unwanted marriage at the age of 13 and the many daring escapes and escapades that followed. Breaking out of the traditional world that confined her, she lived the life of a runaway in cosmopolitan Mogadishu, before escaping abroad. She now lives in the United States.

Mariama Bâ

SENEGAL

was born in Dakar in 1929 and was educated at the Ecole Normal for girls in Rufisque. She was given a traditional Muslim upbringing by her maternal grandparents, studying the Qur'an during school holidays. She became a pioneer of women's rights and was involved in several Senegalese women's organizations. It was her commitment to eradicating inequalities between men and women in Africa that led her to write *So Long a Letter*. This novel – her first – catapulted her onto the African literary scene, where she received much acclaim and admiration. Originally written in French, it was translated into 16 languages and won the first Noma Award for Publishing in Africa.

A schoolteacher and inspector by profession, Bâ believed the writer to have a 'sacred mission' to strike out 'at the archaic practices, traditions and customs that are not a real part of our precious cultural heritage'. Bâ died tragically in 1981 in Dakar after a long illness, just before her second novel *Le Chant Ecarlate* appeared.

Abena Busia

GHANA

was born in 1953, the daughter of Dr Kofi Busia, former Prime Minister of Ghana. She was educated in Ghana, Holland, Mexico and England, and is author of the book *Testimonies of Exile*. Some of her poems have also been included in *Summer Fires: New Poetry from Africa* (Heinemann, Oxford).

Jung Chang

CHINA

was born in Yibin, Sichuan Province, China, in 1952. She was a Red Guard briefly at the age of 14 and then worked as a peasant, a 'barefoot doctor', a steel-worker, and an electrician before becoming an English-language student and, later, an assistant lecturer at Sichuan University. She left China for Britain in 1978 and was subsequently awarded a scholarship by York University, where she obtained a PhD in Linguistics in 1982 – the first person from the People's Republic of China to receive a doctorate from a British university. Jung Chang lives in London and teaches at the School of Oriental and African Studies, London University.

Andrée Chedid
EGYPT

was born in 1921 – of Egyptian-Lebanese parents – in Cairo. She grew up in Egypt and has drawn on that background for her themes, her settings and much of her imagery. Many of her novels and plays are set in Egypt: the Ancient Egypt of Pharoah Akhnaten, the Egypt of the Fourth Century AD, and the present-day Egypt of ordinary people. However, she crossed many cultural as well as temporal boundaries in her work. Her first poems, published in Cairo, were written in English, and since 1946 she has lived mainly in France and written in French. A prolific writer, she has published 22 volumes of poetry, seven novels, five plays and other writings, and has won many major literary awards.

Domitila Barrios de Chungara
BOLIVIA

was born in the mining village of Siglo XX in the Bolivian Andes in 1937. Her mother died when she was nine, and she became responsible for raising her four sisters in extreme poverty. Her father, an activist in the Movement Nacionalista Revoluciona-rio, lost his job because of his political activities. When Domitila grew up she married a tin miner and had seven

children. During this time she became involved in the struggle of the Bolivian tin miners, organizing the women into an active force, and becoming herself a militant women's leader. Domitila recorded her development as a popular leader with the help of Brazilian journalist and social anthropologist Moema Viezzer. The result was the book *Let Me Speak!*

Anita Desai
INDIA

was born in 1937; her father was Bengali and her mother German, and she was educated in Delhi. Her published work includes *Clear Light of Day*, which was shortlisted for the 1980 Booker Prize; *Fire on the Mountain*, for which she won the Royal Society of Literature's Winifred Holtby memorial prize and the 1978 National Academy of Letters Award; *In Custody*, which was shortlisted for the 1984 Booker Prize; *Baumgartner's Bombay* and *The Village by the Sea*. Currently she divides her time between India and the US where she is teaching on a creative writing programme at the Massachusetts Institute of Technology. Her latest book is *Journey to Ithaca*, published in 1995.

Shashi Deshpande
INDIA

was born in 1938 in Dharwar and educated in Bombay. She now lives in Bangalore. Her short stories were first published in various English periodicals in India, and have now appeared in four collections: *The Legacy, The Miracle, It Was the Nightingale* and *It Was Dark*, all published by Writers' Workshop, Calcutta. She has also written five novels including *That Long Silence*.

Nawal El Saadawi
EGYPT

was born in the Egyptian village of Kafr Tahla in the 1930s. Refusing to accept the limitations imposed by both religious and colonial oppression on most women of rural origin, she trained as a doctor of medicine and rose to become Egypt's Director of Public Health. She began writing 30 years ago, producing novels and short stories, and in 1972 published her first study of Arab women's problems and their struggle for liberation, *Women and Sex*. She has suffered at the hands of the Egyptian censors, was forced to shift publication of her works to Beirut, and dismissed from the Ministry of Health. Along with other leading Egyptian intellectuals, she was imprisoned by

President Sadat. She writes in Arabic, but has published several books in English, including *Woman at Point Zero, The Hidden Face of Eve, Death of an Ex-Minister, She Has No Place in Paradise* and *Fall of the Imam.* Nawal El Saadawi is currently teaching in the US.

Fanny Fierro
ECUADOR

was born in 1939 and as well as being a poet is a doctor of literature and linguistics from Pontificia Universidad Católica del Ecuador, Quito. She is currently a visiting professor at Willamette University in Oregon, teaching Spanish language and literature, and Latin American culture and civilization. Her publications include numerous articles, essays and literary studies published in journals, newspapers and magazines on subjects such as women's issues, human rights, children's rights, indigenous and grassroots movements, and linguistics. She has received numerous awards, among them The Gabriela Mistral National Poetry Award and the National Poetry Award in Ecuador.

Bessie Head
BOTSWANA

was born in 1937 in South Africa, daughter of a white mother and a black father. She migrated to Botswana in her early twenties, rejecting the legalities and ethics of apartheid which had forced her – as 'a Coloured' – to be brought up in foster homes and restricted her teaching to a

segregated school. She took her only son across the border and waited 14 years to gain Botswanan citizenship. An extraordinary and prolific writer, Bessie Head wished to be ordinary, to live simply among villagers, away from political tensions and élitist domination. Her writing reflects this interest, but also her own traumatic experience of rejection. Bessie Head's many books include: *When Rain Clouds Gather, Maru, Serowe: Village of the Rain Wind, A Question of Power, Tales of Tenderness and Power, A Woman Alone* and *Gesture of Belonging.* She died in 1986.

Margaret Hooks

Born in Belfast, this Irish writer now lives in Mexico City. As a foreign correspondent for the Irish Times she covered the war in Guatemala in the 1980s. She is author of *Guatemalan Women Speak* (CIIR London 1991, EPICA Washington 1993), a collection of interviews with Guatemalan women which includes an introduction by Rigoberta Menchu. Ester, whose interview appears in this book, is a founder member of GAM – a mutual support group composed of relatives of Guatemala's thousands of 'disappeared' people. Margaret Hooks is also the translator of the

autobiography of Austrian feminist and psychoanalyst Marie Langer, *From Vienna to Managua* (Free Association Books, London 1989). Her most recent work is the award-winning biography *Tina Modotti: Photographer and Revolutionary* (Pandora/HarperCollins, London 1993).

Anees Jung
INDIA

was born in Hyderabad, India. She was brought up in strict *purdah,* but later went on to study at Osmania University and the University of Michigan, Ann Arbor, where she took a Master's degree in sociology and American studies. She has been the editor of a magazine, *Youth Times,* and has written for several of the world's major newspapers. Apart from *Unveiling India,* she has also written *When a Place Becomes a Person* and *Poems and Prose.* She lives in NewDelhi.

Kebbedesh
TIGRAY

was born in 1950, into a peasant family. The feudal system meant that the poor subsistence peasant farmers had most of their produce taken from them; peasant women were at the bottom of the hierarchy, with absolutely no rights. Raped at the age of seven by her much older husband, she led the life of a runaway and prostitute before returning to her region to join the Tigrayan People's Liberation Front (TPLF) in its fight against both feudalism and the Ethiopian Government. She was interviewed by Jenny Hammond of Third World First for the book *Sweeter Than Honey: Testimonies of Tigrayan Women*, published in 1989.

Jane King
SAINT LUCIA

was born in 1952 and currently teaches at the Sir Arthur Lewis Community College in Castries. In recent years she has published stories and poems in several regional journals and anthologies. A selection of her poems is included in the anthology *Confluence: Nine Saint Lucian Poets*. A collection of her poetry is forthcoming.

Clarice Lispector
BRAZIL

was born in 1925 of Ukrainian Jews who emigrated to Brazil when she was two months old. Until she was 12, her family lived in poverty in the Northeastern state capitals of Maceió and Recife. In 1934 her mother died and three years later the family moved to Rio de Janeiro where the young Clarice decided to become a writer. In the 1940s she attended law school while working as an editor for a press agency and afterwards as a reporter for a Rio daily. In 1944 she published her first novel, *Near to the Wild Heart*. She spent the next 15 years writing and living abroad, then returned to Rio after her marriage broke up and published *Family Ties*, *Apple in the Dark*, *The Foreign Legion* and *The Hour of the Star*. Clarice Lispector became one of Brazil's most influential writers, and has been

recognized as the greatest modern short-story writer in the Portuguese language, and a novel writer of exquisite precision and philosophical importance. Her recurring theme was the fragility of peace and order, and the swarming of temptations in unlikely places. She died in 1977.

Gita Mehta
INDIA

was educated in India and at Cambridge University. She has worked on a number of television films and is the author of the highly acclaimed *Raj*, *A River Sutra* as well as *Karma Cola*. She is married with one son and divides her time between India, London and New York. She has written, produced and directed a number of documentaries for American, British and European television companies.

Gabriela Mistral
CHILE

was born in Montegrande, Chile in 1889. In 1945 she won the Nobel Prize for Literature, the first Latin American to do so. The first comprehensive anthology in English, *A Gabriela Mistral Reader* (White

Pine Press), appeared in 1993. Among her principal works are *Desolación* (1922), *Lecturas para mujeres* (1932) and *Poema de Chile* (1967).

Kishwar Naheed
PAKISTAN

was born in 1943. A feminist poet who ceaselessly challenges patriarchy both in words and deeds, Kishwar Naheed was for several years Editor of the prestigious monthly *Maah-i-Nau*. During this time she was on 30 occasions charged with offences, including 'obscenity' when she published an abridged version of Simone de Beauvoir's *The Second Sex*. Perhaps the most prolific Urdu poet of her generation, her writing became more political as repression of women intensified following the deposing of President Zulfihar Ali Bhutto. Her poems range from traditional love poems to those dealing with hysterectomy, male chauvinism, censorship, Western intervention in Pakistan and a host of feminist issues. Her work includes several volumes of poetry: *Lips That Speak*, *Unnamed Journey*, *Poems*, *Amidst Reproaches*, *The Colour Pink Within a Black Border* and *Complete Poems*. Her prose work *Woman 'twixt Dreams and Dust* deals with Pakistani women's issues in depth.

Suniti Namjoshi

INDIA

was born in Bombay in 1941, leaving India
for the West in 1968. She has published
numerous poems, fables, and articles and
reviews in anthologies, collections and
Women's Studies journals in India, Canada
and Britain. Her books include *Feminist
Fables, The Conversations of Cow, Aditi and
the One-Eyed Monkey, The Blue Donkey Fables,
Because of India: Selected Poems, The Mothers
of Maya Diip* and *Saint Suniti and the
Dragon.* Suniti Namjoshi is renowned for
her command of the modern fable *genre,*
her humour and originality. She lives in
Devon, England, and is currently working
on *Building Babel,* which is about the
process of building a culture. The final
chapter will be put on the Internet as a
kind of building site to which others
will contribute.

Grace Nichols

GUYANA

was born in 1950 and is a novelist and
children's writer as well as a poet. She has
published a novel, *Whole of the Morning Sky,*
but is best known for her collections of
poetry: *i is a long-memoried woman* which
won the Commonwealth Poetry Prize in
1983, *The Fat Black Woman Poems* and *Lazy
Thoughts of a Lazy Woman.* She reads a selection of her poems on *Contemporary
Literature on Cassette* and *Come From That
Window Child.*

O Chonghui

KOREA

was born in Seoul in 1947. She made her
literary debut in 1968 with a tale of
tortured adolesence – *The Toyshop Woman.*
She has since won two of Korea's most
prestigious literary prizes, the Yi Sang
Award in 1979 for *Evening Games* and the
Tongin Award, in 1982 for *The Bronze
Mirror* – an extract from which appears in
this collection. In both her technique and
subject matter, O is one of the most
challenging of contemporary Korean
writers, using flashbacks, streams of
consciousness and a variety of narrative
viewpoints.

Mrinal Pande

INDIA

was born in 1946 in Madhya Pradesh,
Central India, daughter of the popular
Hindi novelist Shivani. She read English
literature at the University of Allahabad
and later taught the subject there and at
the University of Delhi. Mrinal Pande is
known for her incisive and thought-
provoking writings on contemporary
women's issues in India, and is the author
of *Daughter's Daughter, Separate Journeys* and
several short stories and plays. She is a
professional journalist and writes and
presents for radio and television. From
1984 to 1987 she was Editor of the popular
women's magazine *Vama.* She was
appointed to the Indian Government's
National Commission on Self-Employed
Women and has been responsible for
enquiring into the conditions of work, the
experience, and the contribution to the
national economy of self-employed
women, such as hawkers, business women,
rag pickers and domestic helpers. She edits
the Hindi language weekly *Saptahik
Hindustan* and lives in New Delhi.

Violeta Parra
CHILE

was born in 1904. A folklorist and poet, she is without a doubt one of the most resonant Latin American figures and one of the most important in Chilean popular culture. She also distinguished herself as a popular singer and author of lyric works, among them *Al Son los Dolores y Décimas - Autografía en Verso*. With the passing of time, Violeta Parra is being recognized for her creativity in the field of the lyric. She died in 1967.

Amelia Blossom Pegram
SOUTH AFRICA

was born in Cape Town. She trained as a teacher at Hewat Training College, and later studied at the University of Cape Town, the Guildhall School of Music and Drama in London, and the University of Louisville, Kentucky. She is widely published and translated. Her books are *Deliverance: Poems for South Africa* and *Our Sun Will Rise*.

Giovanna Pollarolo
PERU

was born in 1955 and is one of a generation of innovative, young Peruvian poets. *Entre Mujeres Solas,* her first published text, came out in 1991.

Fahmida Riaz
PAKISTAN

was educated at Sindh University and went on to become Editor of the magazine, *Awaaz.* During the Martial Law Regime, 14 court cases of sedition were filed against the magazine, one of which carried a death penalty. She escaped to India while on bail and lived there for seven years with her husband and two children. After the restoration of democracy she returned to Pakistan and served as Director General of Pakistan's National Book Council. Her book *The Body Lacerated* caused tremendous controversy because of its uninhibited and vigorous exploration of female sexuality. Fahmida Riaz's success as a lyricist is widely acknowledged. Her published works include: *My Crime is Proven, Will You Not See the Full Moon?, Sun, Stones that Speak* and *I Am a Statue of Clay*.

Alifa Rifaat
EGYPT

is in her mid-fifties and has spent all her life in the Arab world, immersed in the traditions and culture of Islam. She was brought up in Egypt, a devout Moslem, strictly adhering to the Islamic way of life and well-versed in the Qur'an. Her education and a possible future career in art were curtailed when she married – her parents' alternative to university. A widow, she now lives in Cairo with her three children. Largely divorced from Western influences, speaking and writing only Arabic, Alifa Rifaat allows the reader a rare and enlightening glimpse at women's condition in a male-dominated environment. *Distant View of a Minaret* was first published in English in 1983, by Quartet Books. Two of the stories from that collection have been broadcast on BBC Radio 3.

Amina Saïd

TUNISIA

was born in 1953 in Tunis. Her books of poetry include *Paysages*, *Nuit friable* and *Métamorphose et la vague*.

Bulbul Sharma

INDIA

was born in 1952. She was educated in Madhya Pradesh and at Jawaharlal Nehru University, Delhi, following which she studied Russian literature in Moscow. A well-known painter and printmaker, she has had several solo and group exhibitions of her work; she also regularly conducts nature and art workshops for Jagriti, an organization working with street-children in Delhi. A keen bird-watcher, Bulbul has written a book on Indian birds and one on Indian trees. She is also the author of a book of stories, *My Sainted Aunts*.

Luisa Valenzuela

ARGENTINA

was born in 1938 in Buenos Aires. Literature was an important part of her upbringing: her mother, Luisa Mercedes Levinson, was a well-known Argentine author. Luisa Valenzuela began an early literary career working on the staff of the newspaper *La Nación*. Her fiction can best be characterized as revolutionary. It challenges the validity of social structures and institutions: religion, machismo, marriage and sexual taboos. At a metaphysical, creative level, it promotes the idea of a world understood in terms of everlasting, ever-moving, atemporal energy. Translations of her work include *Strange Things Happen Here*, *Other Weapons*, *Open Door* and *The Lizard's Tale*.

– photographers –

Shahidul Alam
Drik Picture Library, House 58, Road 15 A (New) Dhanmondi,
RA, Dhaka 1209, Bangladesh. Tel: (0) 88 02 328 332
Photo on page 29

Dieter Amsler
Pestalozzistrasse 42, 8200 Schaffhausen, Switzerland.
Tel: (0) 52 624 4751
Photo on page 73

Bruno Barbey
Magnum Photographers, Moreland Buildings, 2nd Floor,
23-25 Old Street, London EC1V 9HL, UK. Tel: (0) 171 490 1771
Photo on page 69

Carol Beckwith
Robert Estall Picture Library, Falson House, 12-14 Swan Street,
Boxford, Sudbury, Suffolk CO10 5NZ, UK.
Tel: (0)1787 210111, Fax: (0)1787 211 440
Photo on page 51

Barnabas Bosshart
Feldstrasse 1a, CH-8370 Sirnach, Switzerland.
Tel: (0) 71 966 3219, Fax: (0) 71 971 3506
Photos on pages 63, 67, 85 and 97.

Martin Brauen
c/o Völkerkundemuseum, Pelikanstrasse 40, 8001 Zurich,
Switzerland.
Tel: (0)1 221 31 91
Photo on page 31

Ed Brouns
Nieuwe Holleweg 25, 6573 DT Beek Ubbergen, Holland.
Photo on page 105

Margaret Courtney-Clarke
Via Maiura 274, Ceccano 03023, Italy.
Tel: 775 629 004, Fax: 775 629 516
Photo on page 59

Mark Edwards
Still Pictures, 199a Shooters Hill Road, Blackheath,
London SE3 8UL, UK. Tel: (0)181 858 8307
Photo on page 23

Sarah Errington
The Hutchison Picture Library, 118 B Holland Park Avenue,
London W11 4UA, UK. Tel: (0)171 229 2743
Photos on pages 83, 107 and 115

Claire Eykerman
Ruse Fraikin 43, 1030 Brussels, Belgium. Tel: (0) 322 216 4323
Photo on page 17

Peter Frey
101 Cours de la Republique, 84210 Pernes, France.
Tel: (0) 16 90 616 586
Photos on pages 61, 65 and 81

Ashvin Gatha
CP 96/Chemin Champ-Jaccoud 2,
CH-1807, Blonay, Switzerland.
Tel: (0) 21 943 4433
Photo on page 53

Willy Germann
Rundstr. 15, CH-8400 Winterthur, Switzerland.
Tel: (0) 52 212 84 40
Photo on page 95

Anne-Marie Grobet
Rte Mandemant 311, 1281 Russin, Switzerland.
Tel: (0)22 754 1652. Fax: (0)22 754 1252
Photo on page 79

Carlos Guarita
Reportage, 28 Norcott Road, London N16 7EL, UK.
Tel: (0)181 806 9803 Fax: (0)181 806 6980
Photo on page 39

Jeremy Hartley
Panos Pictures, 9 White Lion Street, London N1 9PD, UK.
Tel: (0)171 278 1111
Photo on front cover and title page

Adriano Heitmann
PO Box 124, CH-6855 Stabio, Switzerland.
Tel:(0) 91 630 9110 Fax:(0) 91 630 91 11
Photos on pages 27 and 47

T. Hopker
Magnum Photographers, Moreland Buildings, 2nd Floor,
23-25 Old Street, London EC1V 9HL, UK.
Tel: (0)171 490 1771
Photo on page 99

Jeremy Horner
The Hutchison Library, 118b Holland Park Avenue,
London W11 4UA, UK.
Tel: (0)171 229 2743
Photo on page 21

Walter Imber
Weingarten 362, CH-4524 Gunsberg, Switzerland.
Tel: (0)65 771 703, Fax: (0)65 772 401
Photo on page 43

Nasrolah Kasraian
Milkenstrasse 3, CH-3150 Schwarzenburg, Switzerland.
Tel: (0)31 731 0871
Photo on page 87

Barry Lewis
Network Photographers, 3-4 Kirby Streeet, London EC1N 8TS, UK.
Tel: (0)171 831 3633
Photo on page 33

Jenny Matthews
Network Photographers, 3-4 Kirby Street, London EC1N 8TS, UK.
Tel: (0)171 831 3633
Photo on page 91

James Nelson
1ste Sweelinckstrasse 23, NL-1073 CL, Holland.
Tel: (0)31 20 673 8539, Fax: (0)31 20 673 6691
Photo on page 57

Paul O'Driscoll
Impact Photos, 26/27 Great Sutton Street,
London EC1V ODX, UK.
Tel: 0171 251 5091
Photo on page 111

Vivian Olmi
50 ch. de Liaudoz, CH-1009 Pully, Switzerland.
Tel: (0)21 729 4215
Photo on page 93

Marco Paoluzzo
Rue Principale 11, CH-2560 Nidau, Switzerland.
Tel:(0) 32 51 02 93
Photo on page 101

Robert Schmid
Erzbergweg 13, CH-5016 Obererlinsbach, Switzerland.
Tel:(0) 62 844 33 67
Photo on page 103

Raghubir Singh
Colorific! The Innovation Centre,
225 Marsh Wall, London E14 9FX, UK.
Tel: (0)171 515 3000, Fax: (0)171 538 3555
Photo on page 77

Georg Stärk
Seestrasse 316, CH-8810 Horgen, Switzerland.
Tel:(0) 1 725 79 04
Photo on page 49

Tina Tsukada
Zollikerstrasse 263, CH-8008 Zurich, Switzerland.
Tel: (0)1 381 6101
Photo on page 71

Amedeo Vergani
Via Girolamo Emiliani 6, 22046 Merone, Italy.
Tel: (0)31 650 423, Fax: (0)31 650 588
Photos on pages 19, 25, 35 and 41

– acknowledgements –

Assumpta Acam-Oturu: 'Arise to the Day's Toil', from The Heinemann Book of African Women's Poetry, ed. Stella and Frank Chipasula, 1995, Heinemann, Oxford.

Omega Agüero: 'A Man, A Woman', from El Muro de Medio Metro, 1977, Union de Escritores y Artistas de Cuba, Havana.

Ama Ata Aidoo: from Changes, 1991, The Women's Press, London.

Malak'Abd Al Aziz: The Fall, from The Heinemann Book of African Women's Poetry, ed. Stella and Frank Chipasula, 1995, Heinemann, Oxford.

Isabel Allende: from The House of the Spirits, 1985, Jonathan Cape, London and Alfred A Knopf, Inc., New York; from Eva Luna, 1987, Alfred A Knopf Inc., New York.

Aman: from 'Aman. The Story of a Somali Girl', 1994, Bloomsbury, London.

Mariama Bâ: from So Long a Letter, 1980, Nouvelles Editions Africaines, Dakar, Senegal.

Abena Busia: Liberation from The Heinemann Book of African Women's Poetry, ed. Stella and Frank Chipasula, 1995, Heinemann, Oxford.

Jung Chang: from Wild Swans, 1991, HarperCollins, London.

Andrée Chedid: from 'The Long Trial', from Les Corps et les Temps, 1965, Librairie Ernest Flammarion, Paris.

Domitila Barrios de Chungara: from Let me Speak! 1978, Monthly Press Review/Stage 1, London.

Anita Desai: from 'The Accompanist' from Games at Twilight, 1978, Heinemann, Oxford. 'Studies in the Park', also from Games at Twilight, as above. Copyright with author c/o Rogers, Coleridge and White, London.

Shashi Deshpande: from 'My Beloved Charioteer', from The Inner Courtyard, ed. Lakshmi Holmstrom, 1990, Virago, London.

Nawal El Saadawi: from Woman at Point Zero, 1983, Zed Books, London. 'Eternal Love' from Fall of the Imam, 1988, Methuen, London.

Ester: 'Until We Find Them', from Guatemalan Women Speak, 1991, by Margaret Hooks, CIIR, London.

Fanny Fierro: 'Hidden Love', from These are Not Sweet Girls, trans. Sally Cheney Bell, ed. Marjorie Agosin, 1994, White Pine Press, Fredonia, New York.

Bessie Head: from 'The Old Iron Cooking Pot of Europe', from A Woman Alone, 1990, Heinemann, Oxford.

Anees Jung: from Unveiling India, 1987, reproduced courtesy of Penguin Books India, New Delhi.

Kebbedesh: from Sweeter than Honey: Testimonies of Tigrayan Women, 1989, eds Jenny Hammond and Nel Druce, Third World First, Oxford.

Jane King: 'Clichés for an Unfaithful Husband' from The Heinemann Book of Caribbean Poetry, 1992, Heinemann, Oxford.

Clarice Lispector: from The Hour of the Star, 1977, Carcanet Press, Manchester.

Gita Mehta: from Karma Cola, 1980, Jonathan Cape Ltd, London. Copyright with author c/o Rogers, Coleridge and White, London.

Gabriela Mistral: from 'My Mother', from These are Not Sweet Girls, trans. Maria Jacketti, ed. Marjorie Agosin, 1994, White Pine Press, Fredonia, New York.

Kishwar Naheed: 'To Masters of Countries With a Cold Climate' from We Sinful Women, ed. Rukhsana Ahmad, 1991, The Women's Press, London.

Suniti Namjoshi: 'The Gods', from Feminist Fables,1981, Sheba, London.

Grace Nichols: 'A Tropical Death' from The Fat Black Woman's Poems, 1984, Virago, London. 'Tapestry' from Lazy Thoughts of a Lazy Woman, 1989, Virago, London.

O Chonghui: from 'The Bronze Mirror' from Land of Exile, 1993. Reprinted with permission from M E Sharpe, Inc., Armonk, NY, 10504.

Mrinal Pande: from 'Daughter's Daughter', 1993, Mantra Publishing Ltd., London.

Violeta Parra: 'I Thank Life For So Many Gifts' from These are Not Sweet Girls, , trans. Bonnie Shepard, ed. Marjorie Agosin, 1994, White Pine Press, Fredonia, New York.

Amelia Blossom Pegram: 'I Will Still Sing' from Our Sun Will Rise: Poems for South Africa, 1989, Three Continents Press, Colorado.

Giovanna Pollarolo: 'The Grocer's Dream' from These are Not Sweet Girls, trans. and ed. Marjorie Agosin, 1994, White Pine Press, Fredonia, New York.

Fahmida Riaz: 'Come, Give Me Your Hand' from We Sinful Women, ed. Rukhsana Ahmad, 1991, The Women's Press, London.

Alifa Rifaat: 'An Incident in the Ghobashi Household', from Distant View of a Minaret, 1983, Quartet, London.

Amina Saïd: from 'And We Were Born' from Sables funabules, 1988, co-edition Arcantère Editions, France/Ecrits des Forges, Quebec.

Bulbul Sharma: from 'Rites of Passage' from In Other Words, eds Urvashi Butalia and Ritu Menon, 1993, first published by Kali for Women, B1/8 Hauz Khas, New Delhi, then by The Women's Press, London.

Luisa Valenzuela: from 'Up Among the Eagles' from Open Door, 1992, Serpent's Tail, London.

Every effort has been made to trace all copyright holders and to clear reprint permissions. This process has been complicated and if any required acknowledgements have been overlooked it is unintentional. If notified, the publishers will be pleased to rectify any omission in future editions.